The Stoy Hayward Guide to
EFFECTIVE
STAFF
INCENTIVES

The Stoy Hayward Guide to
EFFECTIVE STAFF INCENTIVES

Brian Friedman
MA (Cantab) ACA FTII MIPM

KOGAN
PAGE

First published in 1990
Revised edition 1990

Kogan Page Limited
120 Pentonville Road
London N1 9JN
in association with
Stoy Hayward
8 Baker Street, London W1M 1DA

© Brian Friedman, 1990

British Library Cataloguing in Publication Data

A CIP record for this book is available from the British Library.

ISBN 0-7494-0131-1

Typeset by Saxon Printing Ltd, Derby
Printed and bound in Great Britain by
Richard Clay Ltd. The Chaucer Press, Bungay, Suffolk

CONTENTS

Foreword   *ix*
Preface   *xi*
Acknowledgements   *xiii*
Introduction   **xv**

1   Designing an Incentive Scheme   **1**
Stage 1 – Why introduce a scheme ?   2
Stage 2 – Identifying your objectives   6
Stage 3 – Selecting the participants   8
Stage 4 – Choosing the performance measure   10
Stage 5 – Scheme design   14
Stage 6 – Launch   17
Stage 7 – Post-launch   18
The need for ceremony   19
Quick summary   20

2   Non-cash Incentive Schemes   **21**
Visibility   21
Vouchers   22
The nagging spouse factor   23
The Taxed Award Scheme   23
Overseas conferences   24
Taxation implications   25
Quick summary   25

3   Golden Hellos, Handcuffs, and Handshakes   **26**
Competing for people   26
General background   27
Tax generally   28
Special rules for lump sum payments   28
Golden hellos   28

Golden handcuffs   29
Golden handshakes   30
Practical aspects   31
Redundancy payments   31
National Insurance   32
Restrictive covenants   32
Quick summary   32

4 **Company Cars**   33
The role of the car in incentive planning   33
The employee's position   33
Car parking and car telephones   37
The choice of car   38
The employer's position   39
Contract hire v. finance leasing   41
Quick summary   42

5 **Other Fringe Benefits**   43
General   43
Cafeteria benefits   43
Use of company assets   44
Luncheon facilities   45
Medical insurance   46
Cheap loans   46
Accommodation   47
Tax-free relocation   48
Telephone allowances   48
Suggestion schemes   48
Long-service awards   49
Sporting facilities   49
Nursery facilities   49
Quick summary   51

6 **The Role of Pensions in Incentive Planning**   52
General   52
Final salary schemes   54
Money purchase scheme   55
Executive 'top-hat' schemes   56
Additional voluntary contributions (AVCs)   57
Salary and bonus sacrifices   58
Additional benefits   59
Personal pensions   60
Unapproved pension arrangements   61
Portability   62

Contracting out   62
Quick summary   63

7   **Profit-Related Pay**   **64**
Background   64
The basic rules   65
Registration   66
Requirements of a PRP scheme   67
Ascertainment of the distributable pool   67
Ascertainment of profits   68
Cancellation   69
Quick summary   69

8   **Share Incentives Generally**   **71**
Background   71
Incentivising with shares   73
Unapproved schemes   76
General rules   76
Unapproved share options   77
Approved or unapproved?   78
Phantom share options   79
The need for ceremony revisited   80
How to get rich quick!   81
Quick summary   81

9   **Approved Employee Share Schemes**   **83**
Executive share option schemes   83
Profit-sharing schemes   85
Buy one, get one free   86
Sharesave – you just can't lose   87
Easing the admin burden – at no extra cost   90
Quick summary   91

10   **ESOP**   **92**
Background   92
How does an ESOP work?   94
Qualifying ESOPs   95
Qualifying or non-qualifying?   96
ESOPs as a poison pill   97
Captive shares   98
A new tool in corporate finance   99
ESOPs as a marketmaker   99
An alternative to flotation   100
Quick summary   100

Appendix 1   The Taxed Award Scheme   102
Appendix 2   Suggestion Schemes   104
Appendix 3   Registration Form for Profit-Related Pay   106
Appendix 4   Employee Share Schemes – ABI Guidelines   111
Appendix 5   Employee Share Schemes – NAPF Guidelines   120
Appendix 6   Employee Share Schemes – Stock Exchange
              Requirements   123
Appendix 7   Employee Share Option Scheme – Inland
              Revenue Specimen Rules   125
Appendix 8   Savings Related Share Option Scheme –
              Inland Revenue Specimen Rules   134
Appendix 9   Profit-Sharing Scheme – Inland Revenue
              Specimen Trust Deed and Rules   144

Stoy Hayward   162

Index   167

Foreword

Effective Staff Incentives is an invaluable guide for enlightened companies who recognise that a key factor in business success is the involvement of all employees through comprehensive reward packages.

National pay awards which undermined linkage with the success of individual enterprises are fast fading away. We can progressively move to a high reward/high performance and productivity approach to remuneration instead of a low pay approach to competitiveness.

I was surprised by the vast range of options presented by the author. I am sure that those who use this book will find it most helpful to have the full array of benefits in front of them, to assist in tailoring their own company's or client's packages.

Effective leadership in winning organisations is about producing extraordinary performance from ordinary people. Effective incentives have a key role to play in this process. Those who make full use of this book can therefore be major contributors to the pursuit of excellence.

Walter Goldsmith
Former Director General (1979–84)
Institute of Directors
Co-author of The Winning Streak

Preface

The first few months of the 1990s have already demonstrated the increasing significance being placed by employers on the provision of effective staff incentives.

Increasingly, companies are facing up to the reality of a shrinking labour market by devising incentives designed to attract and retain working mothers. Some companies such as Abbey National and Legal & General are prepared to pay special allowances to women returning to work. Others, such as Midland Bank, are establishing workplace nurseries. Intense lobbying has resulted in this latter benefit being made tax free from 6 April 1990 although the tax relief is by no means as generous as many had hoped.

Employee share ownership continues to enjoy widespread cross-party political support and welcome improvements have been made to both ESOPs and Sharesave schemes. As a result, the trend towards employee share ownership seems virtually unstoppable as more and more companies offer their employees a share of the action.

The increasing competition for skilled employees is likely to encourage employers to emulate their US counterparts by offering flexible compensation packages. Colloquially known as 'cafeteria benefits', this system allows employees to choose their preferred benefits from a pre-determined 'menu'. Although cafeteria benefits will inevitably have an administrative cost, it is likely that the ability to offer bespoke remuneration packages will become a major factor in the recruitment market.

The design of effective staff incentives is limited only by the boundaries of one's own imagination. This book is intended to be a short distillation of the many effective staff incentives currently available. It does not purport to be comprehensive but it does hope to provide food for thought.

Brian Friedman
August 1990

Acknowledgements

The author wishes to acknowledge with gratitude the assistance given by the following:

Sandy Johnson for deciphering and typing the manuscript. Mike Owens and Tom Digby (both formerly of Inland Revenue Technical Division – Employee Share Schemes) and Phil Leiwy all of Stoy Hayward for their constructive advice on the employee share scheme aspects; Glen McKeown of Stoy Hayward pension consultancy for his input to Chapter 6 – the role of pensions in incentive planning; David Cohen of Paisner & Co. for permission to quote from his survey – *Employee Participation in Flotations*; Monks partnership for permission to use material from their survey – *SAYE Option Plans in Practice*; Willow Cartoons for bringing a touch of humour to the text; colleagues (too numerous to mention individually) at Stoy Hayward for their helpful advice and criticism; Pauline Goodwin at Kogan Page; and the Inland Revenue, the Stock Exchange, the Association of British Insurers and the National Association of Pension Funds for permission to reproduce the material included in the appendices. And especially Fran, Emma and Jonathan.

Introduction

This book has been written as a practical guide rather than as a technical textbook. Its purpose is to examine the different possibilities open to companies wishing to motivate or 'incentivise' their staff.

No excuse is made for the word 'incentivise' despite the fact that the author was once told that only Americans 'verbalise' nouns! This author, however, defies any reader to come up with a term which better reflects the concept of motivating employees through incentives than the single word 'incentivise'. Every time the word is mentioned people shudder; but they do understand precisely what it means.

This draws an analogy with incentive scheme planning generally. The effectiveness of any employee incentive scheme depends more on its perception than on the actual scheme itself. Communication is all-important and the use of well-chosen words and phrases is essential to ensure that employees understand the targets set for them and the rewards that their efforts can generate.

Most professional advisers in this area fall into one of two categories. On the one hand are the reward and benefit consultants who, although experienced in the concepts of incentive scheme design, may be unable to undertake the drafting of scheme rules or comment on the detailed taxation implications. On the other hand are the lawyers and draftsmen who will carry out the design and implementation of an incentive scheme in a mechanistic fashion without consideration of the subtle motivational factors that can make or break an incentive scheme.

This book hopes to combine both the human resource and the technical aspects of employee incentive schemes so as to provide, perhaps for the first time, a complete manual for incentive scheme design.

The book is intended to examine both the motivational and fiscal implications of designing and running an incentive scheme. It covers the whole range of schemes from simple cash bonus schemes to the most complex share scheme and ESOP arrangements. That having been said, it has been written as a general guide. Any course of action will depend upon the particular circumstances of your business and you are strongly advised to obtain specific professional advice before implementing any scheme. Neither the author nor Stoy Hayward can assume legal responsibility for the accuracy of any particular statement in this book.

The law is as stated at 1 August 1990.

Chapter 1

Designing an Incentive Scheme

Overview

Most employers will operate an employee incentive scheme of one form or another. The informal 'pat-on-the-back and here's £50' approach adopted by many smaller companies is as much an incentive scheme as the most detailed performance-related bonus scheme operated by any multi-national. It is, of course, a question of

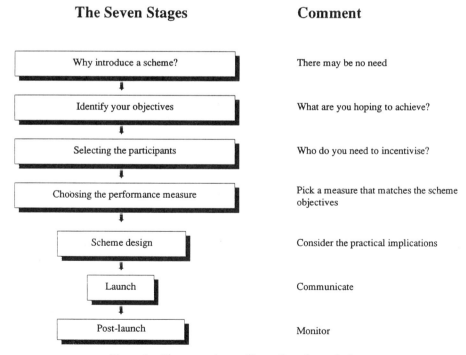

The Seven Stages   **Comment**

The Seven Stages	Comment
Why introduce a scheme?	There may be no need
Identify your objectives	What are you hoping to achieve?
Selecting the participants	Who do you need to incentivise?
Choosing the performance measure	Pick a measure that matches the scheme objectives
Scheme design	Consider the practical implications
Launch	Communicate
Post-launch	Monitor

Figure 1 The seven stages of incentive scheme design

'horses for courses' and when designing an incentive scheme for your own employees it is imperative to understand what will and what will not work within your own organisation.

Designing an incentive scheme can be split up into seven constituent stages which should each be considered in turn if the incentive scheme is to be a success rather than an outright failure. The seven stages are considered in more detail below but stages can be illustrated diagrammatically as in Figure 1.

Stage 1 – Why introduce a scheme ?

The first issue that must be considered is the rationale for introducing an incentive scheme. What is the scheme meant to achieve? Will more pay achieve results? Why?

Figure 2   Ability, motivation and clarity of task

Performance is not simply a matter of motivation. It will also depend on the ability of the employees concerned and their understanding of the tasks. All three must be kept in balance if performance is to be maximised. The interaction of ability, clarity of task, and motivation can be represented diagrammatically as in Figure 2. If only one or two of the three constituent performance factors are present the results can be disastrous. Table 1 indicates the results for all eight possible combinations of ability, clarity of task, and motivation.

It can be seen from this that there is little point in incentivising staff unless the other two factors are already present. In other words the employees must have the necessary ability and must understand what it is that they are required to do. This is a prerequisite to

Table 1   Interaction of three constituent factors

Ability	Clarity of task	Motivation	Result
High	High	High	High performance
High	High	Low	Poor performance
High	Low	Low	Poor and bad performance
High	Low	High	Frustration
Low	High	High	Incompetent performance
Low	High	Low	Incompetent poor performance
Low	Low	High	Incompetent bad performance
Low	Low	Low	Disaster !

incentivising and if the employees in your organisation do not meet these requirements, there is little point in reading any further as the rest of this book starts from this basic assumption!

The next point to consider is the likely effect that any incentive scheme may have on performance. This will depend on both the scope within the business for performance improvement (*headroom*), and the scope within the organisation for the employees to influence that performance (*leverage*).

Organisations with a high degree of headroom may include new businesses, those undergoing a period of rapid change, for example due to the impact of new technology, as well as those businesses that are underperforming, for example due to poor management. Low headroom will typically arise in mature businesses or businesses operating in a sunset industry.

Employees who have the most scope to influence performance will include salesmen, top management, and other individuals whose decisions will have a direct impact on revenue. Central staff and employees whose tasks are equipment-based are likely to have the least scope to influence performance.

It goes without saying that incentive schemes will achieve the greatest results in high headroom, high leverage situations. Conversely, there may be little or no point in introducing an incentive scheme into a low headroom, low leverage situation.

It should not be forgotten that pay is not the only way of motivating staff and it may be that there are other more cost-effective methods available. For example, while many employees change jobs to achieve a higher salary it is not always true to say that salary is the reason they decided to leave their old job. Often it is the non-financial aspects that create the environment in which employees start looking for alternative work. Rectifying this situation can be as efficient as any cash incentive scheme.

Non-financial factors which ought to be considered as an alternative (or a complement) to introducing an incentive scheme include better training, a defined career structure, the introduction of better machinery and office equipment, a more pleasant working environment, a friendlier social atmosphere, and similar factors. Even the best designed incentive scheme will fail if the employees are not content with the work environment in which they are expected to perform.

So before deciding to introduce an incentive scheme, consider the rationale for its introduction and whether alternative solutions may be preferable. Remember, once a scheme has been introduced it can become extremely difficult to discontinue it. Employees who have become used to receiving substantial incentive payments are unlikely to be impressed if these stop unless a similar or more attractive remuneration package is introduced. In many cases the only way to

EVEN THE **BEST DESIGNED INCENTIVE SCHEME** WILL FAIL IF THE EMPLOYEES ARE NOT CONTENT WITH THE **WORK ENVIRONMENT**....

discontinue an incentive scheme is to buy it out with an acceptable alternative. It is seldom wise unilaterally to discontinue an attractive (from the employee's point of view) incentive scheme and it may even amount to constructive dismissal and a breach of the employment contract.

For this reason it is important to estimate the costs of operating the incentive scheme both if it works and if it does not. It is often a good idea to put a fixed 'cap' or 'ceiling' on the scheme so that the company's obligations under the scheme are limited. This device is particularly important if you operate in a business that can experience 'windfall' profits. If the profits are truly 'windfall' then by definition they will not have arisen through the efforts of the employees and as such should be excluded in determining incentive scheme payments. Unfortunately, by their very nature, windfall profits are impossible to predict and hence would not normally be excluded under the terms of the scheme. By setting an absolute ceiling, you can ensure that the additional liability under the scheme generated by extraneous factors is limited.

Example

An example of, quite literally, windfall profits was the impact of the October 1987 hurricane on the income and profits of firms of loss adjusters, equipment hire companies and the like. The effect of the hurricane was to generate a completely unexpected surge in business for such companies and an open-ended incentive scheme could have become extremely expensive for the employer and provided excessive rewards to the employees concerned.

The argument against having a ceiling is that the employees should be motivated without the risk of that level of motivation being eroded once the ceiling had been reached. Although there is much validity in this argument – employees will certainly tend to relax once the maximum has been reached – this is largely in the context of ceilings that have been set too low. As a general rule, while any target should be achievable, a ceiling should only be achievable in truly exceptional circumstances.

If it is necessary for one reason or another to have a ceiling which is readily achievable, one solution can be to pay a second tranche of incentive payments to the top performing employees. Thus, even if all employees hit the scheme ceiling, there is still an incentive to maintain performance in order to out-perform each other and so earn the additional bonus.

Stage 2 – Identifying your objectives

Whatever the detail of your incentive scheme, it is essential that time is spent beforehand identifying your views and objectives. Once introduced, an incentive scheme will motivate employees towards achieving the targets established by the scheme. With a well-designed scheme these targets are such that their achievement will enable the business to meet its own goals and targets. This is often called 'goal congruence'. A badly designed scheme may still motivate employees to achieve the scheme targets but those targets may differ from the underlying goals and targets of the business. These schemes are regrettably all too common in business today and are often caused by companies setting up employee incentive schemes before they have fully determined their primary corporate objectives.

Incentive schemes therefore must be tailored to meet the corporate objectives and ethos of the company to which they relate. It is not advisable to transpose a scheme which works successfully in one company directly into another company. Every company is different and what works in one environment may have disastrous consequences in another.

There are, however, some general guidelines that will apply whatever the size of your company. The first point to consider is the rationale for introducing an incentive scheme. Put simply, there is no point in designing an employee incentive scheme until you have determined what the scheme is meant to achieve. While this might sound somewhat obvious to someone contemplating installing an incentive scheme for the first time, there are many older but wiser directors who now appreciate this point – that an incentive scheme can easily backfire if the goals of the scheme do not coincide with those of the company.

Example

One example that springs to mind was the retail chain that wished to boost turnover by paying a sales commission to its employees. The scheme was carefully designed so that employees were motivated to increase sales by a generous commission structure. Unfortunately, the company had been so anxious to boost sales it had omitted to examine the full implications of the scheme. The predictable happened – the employees were so keen to increase sales in order to maximise their commissions that they were prepared to heavily discount the price in order to make the sale. As a result sales rocketed but profits took a nose dive.

It must be recognised that there is no ideal incentive scheme which will produce the desired results for all companies. Indeed, it is highly unlikely that one can ever find any scheme that does not have unfortunate side-effects. The best that can be hoped for in designing an incentive scheme is that the positive aspects will be accentuated and the side-effects minimised. This is because most companies will have a series of goals, many of which may prove to be incompatible. Consider, for example, the following corporate goals, all of which are desirable but many of which can become incompatible:

- Increase turnover
- Increase growth
- Raise capital investment
- Increase profits
- Reduce staff turnover
- Ensure staff operate as a team
- Reward individual performance
- Reduce absenteeism
- Increase corporate awareness.

As has been seen, placing undue emphasis on increasing sales turnover can have an adverse effect on profits if sales are discounted as a result. Similarly, if employees or management are paid performance-related bonuses there may be a disincentive to invest in capital projects and undertake research and development expenditure on the basis that it would depress current profits. Another example of incompatibility is between rewarding individual performance and ensuring staff operate as a team. Employees who are commission driven are unlikely to pass opportunities to a colleague if doing so means missing out on potential commission.

Problems of this kind can arise where you have a number of sales-related employees all carrying out identical work. The question then becomes one of whether the employees should be rewarded individually or by reference to results as a team.

Example

In an Estate Agency, there are typically a small number of negotiators with identical roles – namely selling houses. The employer is faced with a dilemma. If each negotiator receives commission based solely on his own efforts, then he is less likely to co-operate with his fellow negotiators, so that some negotiators will eventually end up less busy than others. From the employer's point of view this is unlikely to be an efficient use of resources. Conversely, the employer may decide that teamwork is paramount and may therefore decide to operate a pooled commission structure so that commissions are shared out between the negotiators on some predetermined basis. While this may foster teamwork, it is unlikely to result in negotiators working as hard as they might have done with individual commissions. This is because the effect of each employee's efforts on his own rewards has become diluted and inevitably the more successful negotiators will feel that they are carrying their less successful colleagues. This is likely to lead to a certain level of disharmony in the office.

The earlier comments about sales-related targets backfiring are equally applicable in the example of estate agents. A negotiator who is paid sales-related commission (whether individually or on a group basis) will be tempted to overspend on advertising and promotional activities in order to generate sales even if profits are adversely affected as a result.

The problem of mutually-incompatible goals is unfortunately almost inevitably present and must be recognised as such. In practice, the best solution is for the directors or senior management to set out as many strategic objectives as can be thought of and then to refine the list down to, say, five core objectives. It is then the turn of the scheme designer to ensure that the scheme will motivate employees to meet as many of those five core objectives as possible.

Stage 3 – Selecting the participants

Having decided upon the most pressing corporate objectives, the next step is to determine which employees should be included within the scheme if the corporate goals are to be achieved. As a general rule, there is no point in including in an incentive scheme those employees whose contribution to achieving the corporate objective is likely to be minimal or non-existent. That is not to say that incentive schemes are only appropriate to those individuals who directly influence performance, for example senior management, sales representatives, etc, but rather that there should be a number of different schemes each directly targeted at a certain group of employees in order to ensure that the overall corporate objectives are met.

Some schemes will almost invariably be company-wide, especially where there is a lack of cohesion which senior management wish to eliminate by promoting a greater sense of corporate identity. But most schemes will be tailored to individual operating units. Even within those units it is necessary to decide who should participate. For example, should it be limited to senior management or open to all employees? Should part-timers be included? Should there be an eligibility requirement for length of service and, if so, should the directors have discretion?

Particular problems can arise with new starters and leavers. Should new starters be eligible immediately or at the end of a probationary period of service? Should the entitlement of new starters be phased in over a period of months in order to prevent them reaping the rewards of efforts put in before they joined? Conversely, should leavers have any rights after the date notice is given or received? Indeed, where the scheme pays out on a deferred basis, should ex-employees have any rights after the date of leaving? Should the same rules apply to all leavers or should there be 'clemency clauses' to cover any or all of the following:

- Death
- Disability
- Injury
- Redundancy
- Retirement at normal retirement age
- Maternity
- Mental illness.

In determining who is to be allowed to participate, it is important not to overlook the consequences each decision might have. The introduction of an incentive scheme into one part of the company may have a demotivating effect in other areas, with employees in the excluded areas feeling like second-class citizens in the corporate hierarchy. Particular care must be taken if the central support staff are excluded as they are the employees who typically will have the least direct impact on profits. In many cases it is advisable to recognise this fact by paying a higher basic or discretionary bonus to those employees who by no fault of their own are unlikely to have any material input on profits but whose contribution is vital to successful performance.

Another area where the greatest care must be taken concerns the interaction between the proposed new scheme and existing pay structures. What effect will the scheme have on current gradings and seniority? The position of existing commission earners will also need to be reviewed, especially if the new scheme is intended to replace existing arrangements. Other points to consider are the effect of the scheme on future pay increases and pension arrangements.

Stage 4 – Choosing the performance measure

By this stage the company should have determined its answers to the following questions:

- Why is an incentive scheme beneficial?
- What are we seeking to achieve?
- Who do we need to motivate?

Having considered the *why*, *what*, and *who* of incentivising, the next step is to get down to the nitty gritty of *how*. This is the most crucial stage and the one where potentially expensive mistakes can be made. For, as was stressed before, unless the performance measure closely reflects the corporate objectives, the incentive scheme will almost certainly backfire as employees seek to maximise their earnings under the scheme even to the detriment of the corporate position.

The performance measure chosen should normally be one which the employee can directly affect. Put at its simplest, the target for a salesman should relate to sales whereas the target for a manager should relate to some measure of profits.

There is little or no point in introducing an incentive scheme if there is no direct relationship between the efforts the employee puts in and the rewards he gets out. If hitting the target is beyond the immediate control of the employee, he is unlikely to be motivated to perform by the introduction of the scheme. That is not to say that the employee will not be delighted if targets are met or dismayed if targets cannot be achieved, but he is unlikely to see the rewards of the incentive scheme as being anything other than remote and hence of no particular concern to him.

Example

A quoted company needing to revive its flagging fortunes decided to introduce an incentive scheme to revitalise performance. The senior management of the company highlighted three core objectives which the incentive scheme was to be targeted at, namely:

- increase branch profits
- increase customer satisfaction
- reduce staff turnover.

The company introduced an extremely generous scheme under which branch managers and staff were offered bonuses linked to the rise in the company's share price. The scheme was intended to run for five years and the bonuses were to be paid at the end of the five-year period calculated by reference to the increase in share price over that period.

The scheme was an unmitigated disaster. It does not matter how hard a branch manager or salesman works – he is not going to affect the company's share price. Although the branch manager may be able to make a significant impact on branch profits, the results of the branch are likely to be a drop in the ocean compared to group profits as a whole. Group profits will be affected by the totality of the profits of all its operations. They will also be affected by uncontrollable factors such as exchange differences, interest rates, etc. Further, there is no direct relationship between profits and share price. The share price will be governed by factors so far removed from the performance of any branch manager as to completely destroy any incentive element. These extraneous factors will include the economic outlook, market conditions, bid speculation, and a myriad of others.

The end result was that the introduction of the scheme failed to motivate employees to work harder or give better customer satisfaction. The fact that the share price rose during the period was welcome news to the employees and correspondingly expensive to the company. It did not, however, motivate the employees to perform.

The third core objective, reducing staff turnover, is also deserving of analysis. Under the terms of the scheme, the employees' share-price-related bonus was only payable at the end of a five-year period. The intention was that the deferred nature of the bonus would dissuade employees from leaving as that would mean sacrificing their bonus.

Correctly structured, deferred bonus schemes (also known as 'golden handcuffs') can be a highly efficient method of reducing staff turnover. But in this instance, the scheme not only did not work, it actually backfired. The problem was that the employees were effectively split into two distinct categories. On the one hand were the 'high fliers' who were ambitious and determined to climb the career ladder to senior management. On the other hand were the 'career managers' who were loyal and solid but scarcely leadership material. Although it had not been identified at the outset, the staff turnover problem related to the high-fliers who were frequently being tempted to join rival organisations by better salary packages and enhanced career prospects.

Staff turnover was also a problem for career managers, but here the problem was that the turnover was too low! Many of the career managers were recognised as 'dead wood'. Potential high-fliers felt demotivated as a result of their career paths being blocked and by the poor management skills of the career managers.

The introduction of the deferred bonus had little impact on staff turnover among the high-fliers. The prospect of a large bonus in five years' time was both too remote and too unpredictable. There was no guarantee that the share price would rise over the five-year period and most high-fliers discounted it from their salary package. A deferred bonus does not pay the mortgage and many high-fliers left to join rival companies for a slightly increased salary and enhanced career prospects.

The position was somewhat different for the career managers. They were far less likely to leave than the high-fliers partly because of their lack of ambition and partly because they were less attractive to potential employers. The possibility of a large bonus was an additional incentive to stay, thus exacerbating the problem for the next tier of high-fliers coming through the ranks.

What this example demonstrates is the importance of setting targets that are relevant and meaningful to the employees who are to be incentivised. The correct choice of performance measure is critical if the scheme is to be successful. An inappropriate choice may soon become a very expensive mistake.

It is therefore advisable to review the various business monitors to determine which are the most appropriate to your business. Some of the more common performance monitors are as follows:

- Sales
- Profits
- Length of service
- Return on capital employed
- Share price
- Earnings per share
- Net asset value
- Productivity.

This list is by no means exhaustive and it would be quite wrong merely to select a performance monitor from this list and seek to apply it to your business. The better approach would be to analyse the core objectives and to work from there to determine the performance monitors that most closely relate to your core objectives.

The targets should be as specific as possible and can be set for all categories of employee. For example, a credit controller could be set targets by reference to average age of debtors or debtors as a percentage of sales. Similarly, the chief accountant might be set targets by reference to the production of monthly management accounts.

The selection of an appropriate performance monitor should not be unilaterally made by the employer. If the scheme is to be successful it is important that the employees appreciate, respect, and understand the choice of performance monitor. In many cases, companies will discuss the rationale behind the scheme and the choice of performance monitor with the employees prior to it being implemented.

The necessity for understanding the performance monitor should not be underestimated. Simple terms such as 'profits' can have widely different meanings, and ambiguity over the precise definition of the performance measure has led to many incentive schemes backfiring.

Example

A large group of companies decided to motivate directors in operating subsidiaries by offering them by way of bonus a percentage of profits. Although the scheme was greatly welcomed on its introduction, ambiguity over the meaning of 'profits' resulted in furious rows and ended up by leaving the directors severely demotivated.

The problem lay in the definition of profits. The directors of the operating subsidiaries had assumed the profits referred to were those shown in the monthly management accounts. This figure was calculated before management charges from the parent company, year end audit adjustments, tax and the bonus itself. Unfortunately, the parent company had intended that the bonus should be paid by reference to profits as stated in the audited financial accounts of the subsidiary, which would be after all these items.

Had the meaning of 'profit' been understood at the outset there would not have been a problem. The scheme was not ungenerous and would have been welcomed by the directors. The problem was that their expectations had been raised as a result of the ambiguity and they felt cheated when the actual bonus fell short of what had been anticipated.

For these reasons, it is essential to draw up a formal, written set of scheme rules in which all important words or phrases are defined. For schemes covering a large number of employees it will also normally be helpful to draw up an explanatory booklet.

Not only should the performance monitor be readily understandable by the employees, it should also be respected. If incentive payments are to be calculated by reference to performance against target, then the target should be realistic and achievable. A target which is too high will be ignored and may lead to bad feeling. A target which is too low will not motivate employees to perform. It may even encourage them to relax their performance on the grounds that they must have been performing to excess beforehand.

The most successful schemes are often those that pay out a percentage of the excess over target (possibly subject to an overriding ceiling). As a rule of thumb, the target should be set at 80% of expected performance so that it is triggered by an average performance. The employee should accept that the target is both fair and realistic and once the target has been triggered he will be aware of the direct relationship between effort and reward.

The practical aspects of the choice of performance measure should also be considered carefully. For instance, there is little point in determining a performance measure if the results cannot be readily identified by the current accounting systems or if the results cannot be ascertained quickly. Other questions to be asked are: Are there any commercial considerations which might apply to the publication of such measures and performance against them? How can the results be affected by changes in accounting practices (eg leasing rather than buying equipment)?

Stage 5 – Scheme design

Once the broad outline and parameters of the scheme have been determined, the next stage is to consider the fine points of scheme design. The documentation that is produced should be comprehensive and cover most conceivable eventualities.

The following checklist sets out some of the more important features that should be included in any set of scheme rules.

1. *Definition of terms*
   All words and phrases that have a specific meaning in the context of the company or which are capable of misinterpretation should be clearly defined.
2. *Duration of scheme*
   The scheme rules should normally state the dates on which the scheme starts and terminates. Either the termination date should be fixed in advance or some statement should be made as to the mechanism for terminating the scheme. This could be as simple as 'such date as the directors may in their absolute discretion determine', or may be calculable by reference to a formula (for example, once a pre-set amount has been paid out under the scheme).

3. *Calculation of incentive payment*

   The scheme rules should state quite clearly the mechanism linking the payment of rewards to the achievement of targets. This is likely to be the very essence of the scheme and it is fundamental that the scheme rules should be precise in this regard.

   Examples of suitable wording might include:

   (a) 1% of Sales for the Period in excess of £x.

   (b) £10,000 multiplied by the percentage increase or decrease in Profits for the Profit Period over the Profits for the immediately preceding Profit Period.

   (c) £1,000 less £50 for every day's absence for any reason whatsoever other than Annual Holiday Entitlement.

   The use of capital letters for certain words and phrases in the above example reflects the fact that those terms would normally be specifically defined in the scheme rules.

4. *Distribution of incentive payment*

   Many incentive schemes operate by ascertaining a 'distributable pool' which is then shared between individual employees on some predetermined basis. Although a distributable pool scheme does have the disadvantage of weakening the link between individual performance and individual reward, it can be a useful method of motivating employees to work together as a team rather than merely as individuals.

   A typical distributable pool scheme will ascertain an aggregate amount (for example by reference to the profits or sales income of the business unit concerned) and will then allocate the pool between employees on a formula basis. Examples of an allocation formula might include:

   (a) In proportion to Basic Salary

   (b) In proportion to length of service

   (c) On a points basis by reference to grade or seniority

   (d) Equally.

5. *Floors and ceilings*

   The scheme rules should normally state both the minimum level of achievement before any incentive payment is made and the maximum amount payable (both to any one individual and in total) under the scheme.

6. *Timing of payment*

   The scheme rules should state the dates on which each incentive payment will be made. A performance-related bonus should normally be paid shortly after the end of the relevant period in which the effort was made. For example, monthly sales commission should normally be paid the following month in order to impress upon the employees the direct relationship between effort and reward.

The position is slightly different where more senior staff are involved or where reducing staff turnover is a core objective. In such circumstances, it is often appropriate to pay the incentive bonus in two instalments with the second instalment being deferred for, say, six months. The deferred element of the bonus is only payable if the employee is still employed at the bonus date. The employee is thus 'locked in' by the thought of a bonus which he has earned but is not entitled to until the bonus date.

7. *Cessation of employment*

The scheme rules should also state the position if an employee leaves during the operation of the scheme or if he leaves during the period between the end of the period and the date the bonus is paid. Cessation of employment may be defined for the purposes of the incentive scheme to mean either the actual date of cessation or the date notice of termination of employment is either given or received.

The rules may also provide for clemency clauses to cover cessation of employment in special circumstances such as death, disability, redundancy, etc. They should also clarify the position regarding maternity leave.

8. *Change of control*

It is often helpful for the scheme rules to state what will happen in the event of the company being taken over or sold. Will there be a contractual commitment to continue the scheme or will it terminate automatically on a change in control? What happens if various business operations are sold or new ones purchased and merged into existing operations?

Similarly, it may also be necessary to consider the implications of alterations to the company's share structure (bonus issues, rights issues, subdivisions, etc) or even the implications of (Heaven forbid!) a winding up.

9. *Amendment*

The scheme rules should state the circumstances in which and the extent by which the rules may be varied or amended. The most flexible solution is to allow the directors the power to amend the scheme 'at any time, without formality and at their absolute discretion'. This, however, is unlikely to be welcomed by employees and may be resisted by their Trade Union or other representatives.

10. *General*

The scheme rules should also address a number of other issues and cover such matters as the deduction of PAYE, the impact on pension contributions and the right (or lack of it) to compensation for incentive payments lost in the event of unfair dismissal.

Stage 6 – Launch

Any incentive scheme is only as good as it is *perceived to be* by the employees. The most carefully designed scheme will fail if it is not communicated properly to the employees. Conversely, a less than perfect scheme may be more than adequate if it receives an enthusiastic welcome from employees.

The keynote is communication. The introduction of the scheme must be supported by all interested parties, the rules must be clear and the benefits explained. It is often sensible to sound out employees in advance in order to gauge their reaction. This can be of particular importance where there is Trade Union representation. Care must be taken to explain that the scheme is intended to confer additional rewards for extra performance and as such is intended to ensure that both the company and its employees prosper.

Particular care should be taken where a replacement scheme is being introduced as employees will inevitably be concerned that they could be worse off under the new scheme. If this is indeed the case then it becomes all the more important to explain the rationale for its introduction at an early stage.

If there are doubts about the effectiveness of the scheme it may be wise to 'pilot' the scheme for a few months in a particular division or area. This can have the advantage of enabling management to review the scheme and, if necessary, to modify or withdraw it before introducing it to the workforce as a whole.

The sophistication of the launch and the amount of corporate resources put into it will depend on the size of the scheme, the number of employees covered by it, and their location. For a simple scheme covering no more than a handful of employees it may be sufficient to explain the scheme in one-to-one meetings and to hand over a copy of the scheme rules.

For a slightly larger scheme, it may still be appropriate to explain the scheme in one-to-one meetings. Here, however, it may be more practicable to explain the scheme in the first instance to executives so that they can 'cascade' the information down to their managers and, in turn, their staff. In such circumstances it is usually advisable to prepare an explanatory booklet to complement the scheme rules. The booklet should however stress that it is merely a guide and does not override the detailed rules of the scheme.

Wherever possible, the explanatory booklet should be professionally produced and printed. A glossy cover with the corporate logo is far more likely to impress employees than a few word-processed sheets of paper. It should not be forgotten that the incentive scheme must be sold to the employees if it is to be a success. Like any selling exercise, the quality of the product is soon forgotten if the packaging is second-rate.

Other ways of communicating the scheme to employees include in-house newsletters, posters, group meetings, and personalised letters. In some cases it can even be worth commissioning an explanatory video, although this is only likely to be the case for very large schemes with a disparate workforce.

Stage 7 – Post—launch

The final stage of designing an incentive scheme is the monitoring of the scheme post-launch in order to ensure that it is used to its greatest potential. It is not only the employees who will see a direct relationship between effort and reward. The employer's position is similar – the more effort he puts in to monitoring and communicating the scheme to employees, the greater the rewards in terms of increased employee motivation and hence corporate performance.

Communication is once again the keynote. Targets should be prominently displayed so that all employees are aware of their position and its implications. Many organisations will regularly pin up posters on notice boards showing performance of each group against target. Where the size of the bonus varies between one group and another or if there is a requirement for confidentiality, some companies use humorous code words or phrases. Where there are a series of targets each of which corresponds to cash bonuses, the level of bonus achieved could be called level one, two, three, etc. A more light-hearted alternative would be to use code phrases for the various bonus levels, for example:

Bonus level 1	A pint of beer
Bonus level 2	A magnum of champagne
Bonus level 3	Dinner for two at the Ritz
Bonus level 4	A weekend in Paris
Bonus level 5	A trip on Concorde

This rather aggressive form of incentivising through prominent target-setting will not suit all organisations and may be out of place in more reserved companies. Nonetheless, the underlying concept may still be valid even if implementation is more low-key.

Another point to bear in mind in the post-launch phase is the importance of injecting an element of fun into the proceedings. Some companies keep the sales book in a prominent position, so that the employee going up to enter the details of a sale in the register is noticed (and often cheered) by his colleagues; an even more forthright version of this involves each employee's name being written on a poster: each time the employee hits a target he draws a red star against his name (again, this may not be suitable for all companies); another version involves employees ringing up the 'sale' on a child's plastic cash register. While all of these procedures might sound somewhat trite, they do tend to inject a sense of fun into the daily routine. Provided the employees enter into the spirit of the proceedings, these fun-aspects can be usefully harnessed to generate a feeling of success and hence to boost corporate performance.

The need for ceremony

The same can be said of the 'need for ceremony' in any incentive scheme. One of the problems with cash as a motivator is that it is invisible (this point is dealt with in more detail in Chapter 2). Other employees will typically not know how much their colleagues earn and even the employee may lose track of his incentive payments if they are paid through the payroll in the normal way. Cash unfortunately is easily frittered away and the all-important bonus can soon disappear amidst the bills and domestic expenses of everyday living.

For this reason, it is helpful to inject a degree of ceremony into the presentation of the bonus. In its simplest form, this might mean nothing more than the bonus cheque (net of PAYE) being personally presented to the employee by his manager together with a few well-chosen words of encouragement. If this is not practicable, then the bonus cheque could be sent to the employees concerned together with a short covering note from the manager.

At the other extreme, many sales-orientated organisations will present incentive scheme payments or prizes (see also Chapter 2) at specially organised dinners or luncheons. This may be excessive for many companies, but the basic concept of the need for ceremony is valid and should not be overlooked if the incentive scheme is to realise its full potential.

Once the scheme has been successfully launched it is important to emphasise its importance at appraisal meetings. Employees should be aware that their performance under the scheme will not only affect their immediate rewards but will also be taken into account in the appraisal process and will have a bearing on promotion prospects.

Lastly, remember that all incentive schemes have a limited life. Incentive scheme planning depends on fresh new ideas – schemes quickly become well-established and lose their motivational sparkle. Do not let old incentive schemes run indefinitely. Try to replace old schemes with new ones on a regular basis.

Quick summary

A summary of the more important ground rules for designing an incentive scheme is set out below:

- There is little point in incentivising employees unless they have both the necessary ability and clarity of task.
- Determine the corporate objectives.
- Design a scheme that will help achieve those objectives.
- Ensure that the employees understand how the scheme works.
- The relationship between effort, performance, and reward should be clear.
- Set achievable targets.
- Make the scheme simple – the employee should be able to calculate earnings easily and see that the potential reward is worth the effort.
- The scheme must be perceived by the employees to be fair and equitable.

Chapter 2

Non-cash Incentive Schemes

Visibility

Employee incentives can come in all shapes and sizes. It would be quite wrong to assume that the only efficient incentive is cash. Indeed, many organisations deliberately offer a mix of cash and non-cash incentives.

At first sight this is illogical. Simple economic theory might suggest that the employee will know how best he wants to spend his money and hence will always prefer cash to any other form of incentive. But in reality this is not the case, for a number of reasons.

First, and most important, cash is largely invisible. An employee who receives a £100 bonus will soon forget that he has received an incentive payment and much of the impact of the incentive scheme will have been lost.

On the other hand, if the employee is given a non-cash incentive (for example a voucher for a local store or a paid holiday) he will be forced to spend the incentive payment on something he will remember. The employee thus enjoys little luxuries that would normally be outside his day-to-day budget.

While non-cash incentives do have a useful role to play in any incentive scheme, care should be taken to limit their use to a controllable proportion. Few employees will appreciate being rewarded entirely in non-cash ways and any non-cash element should be carefully monitored to ensure that it does not have a negative effect.

More will be said about visibility in Chapter 4 on company cars, where similar considerations can apply. The remainder of this chapter relates to the way non-cash rewards can be used in an incentive scheme.

Vouchers

Many companies run schemes whereby employees receive non-cash awards for meeting certain targets (for example, vouchers exchangeable for goods at retail stores). The attraction of vouchers is that the employee is forced to spend the award separately from his normal cash transactions. As a result, he will be far more likely to remember the tangible rewards deriving from the incentive scheme.

.... HE WILL BE FORCED TO SPEND THE INCENTIVE PAYMENT ON SOMETHING HE WILL REMEMBER ....

Other companies operate a points system (somewhat akin to the Green Shield Stamp system, whereby employees are awarded points for each target they meet. All employees are given a glossy catalogue setting out the various 'prizes' under the scheme, together with the number of points needed to earn each prize. The employee can either cash in his points for a small prize or save them up towards a more substantial one.

The nagging spouse factor

One of the attractions of the catalogue system is that the rewards are readily ascertainable by the employee's spouse and family as well as by the employee himself. Thus the whole family can look through the prize catalogue and decide which prize they should go for. In this way the whole family becomes part of the incentive process and will be supportive of the employee by actively encouraging him to meet his performance targets.This is sometimes known as the 'nagging spouse' factor since the wife or husband of the employee may be anxious to persuade him or her to work flat out in order to meet targets. It is also called the 'don't come home from the office early, darling' syndrome!

The Taxed Award Scheme

One of the potential problems with a non-cash incentive scheme is that although the rewards are still fully taxable, tax cannot be deducted at source through the PAYE system. Broadly speaking, PAYE only applies to cash payments: it does not cover non-cash payments such as vouchers and prizes. As a result employees who receive prizes under an incentive scheme may also end up with a tax bill in respect of the value of the prize. This is scarcely likely to endear the prize to the employee who may have been under the impression that the award was tax free.

This problem can be even more difficult where a company provides non-cash incentives to employees of a third party. It is quite common for manufacturers to provide incentive awards to the employees of their distributors in order to encourage sales. It is rare in these circumstances for the employees to appreciate that the 'prize' they have 'won' may come complete with its own tax liability.

In order to help organisations wishing to award non-cash incentives under an incentive scheme, the Inland Revenue have established a procedure known as the Taxed Award Scheme. Under this scheme the organisation enters into a written contract with the Inland Revenue to the effect that it will promise to pay the employee's tax liability on his behalf. It is now possible for the scheme to cover both the employee's higher rate and basic rate tax liability. However, most schemes are still restricted to the basic rate liability only. Thus the employee does not have to pay any tax in respect of the prize, other than in those (relatively few) cases where he is a higher rate taxpayer.

Because the organisation is paying the employee's tax liability on his behalf, the value of the prize has to be grossed up to reflect both the value of the prize and the corresponding tax liability. For example, if an employee is awarded a prize with cost to the employer of £75, the value of that prize grossed up for income tax will be £100 and the tax payable by the employer (under a basic rate scheme) at the current 25% basic rate of tax will be £25. A basic rate taxpayer will have no further tax liability, but a higher rate taxpayer will be required to pay a further £15 tax.

Further details regarding the Taxed Award Scheme are set out in Appendix I.

Overseas conferences

Many companies reward their best employees by hosting overseas conferences or seminars for those staff (often together with their partners) who achieve predetermined performance targets.

Again, the question could be asked, 'Why spend a substantial amount hosting an overseas conference when on any rational basis the employees would prefer cash to spend as they wish?' The answer is that the various factors described above – including visibility and the nagging spouse factor – combine to make the overseas conference a far more efficient incentive than cash could ever be.

Example

Consider for example a company that decides to award its 25 top salesmen with an all-expenses paid trip to a Caribbean 'conference'.

The first step in the incentive process is to announce the destination and to provide the salesmen with a glossy brochure giving full details of the trip, including the five-star hotels being stayed in, etc.

Incentive conferences tend to be lavish in the extreme. This is because it is important that the quality of the trip is far in excess of the normal spending power of the employee so that the impact of the incentive on performance is maximised. The use of the brochure brings the nagging spouse factor into play as both partners dream of the possibility of winning the trip.

The 25 top performing salesmen win the incentive prize and go off to the Caribbean with their wives and husbands. This brings the visibility factor into play. Everyone in the organisation knows who are the winners. The losers also stand out – by their very presence in the office.

The winners inevitably become more close-knit during the course of the conference and new friendships are formed. An élitist clique is formed. When the winners return from the conference the visibility factor comes into play once more. The winners are sun tanned, have in-jokes and are busy showing off their photos. All this will impress on the losers the amount they lost by not meeting the peformance targets, and should encourage them to work even harder next year.

The winners, on the other hand, will also be motivated to win a place on next year's trip to an equally exotic (but different) destination. They are not motivated by the same feelings that affected the losers; rather they are motivated by their memories of a wonderful trip and the realisation that next year's trip will be even better!

Taxation implications

The provision of an overseas conference is likely to be viewed with suspicion by the Inland Revenue. They will normally seek to assess the attendees on a benefit-in-kind calculated by reference to the cost incurred by the company in providing the benefit.

To the extent that attendance at the conference is part and parcel of the employee's duties, no assessable benefit should arise. If the conference has a reasonable work content the Inland Revenue will allow an apportionment of the cost to be made in respect of the business element. However, in practice, the Inland Revenue view overseas conferences with an increasing degree of suspicion as the locations become more exotic.

Quick summary

A summary of the more important aspects of non-cash incentive schemes is set out below:

- Non-cash incentives can be far more powerful than cash payments.
- The non-cash element should however be monitored to ensure it does not have a negative effect.
- Voucher schemes can involve the whole family thus increasing the motivational impact on the employee.
- The Inland Revenue Taxed Award Scheme can ensure most employees do not receive a tax bill in respect of their 'prize'.
- The business element of overseas conferences should not be taxable.

Chapter 3

Golden Hellos, Handcuffs, and Handshakes

Competing for people

So far, much has been said regarding the use of incentives to elicit a high standard of performance from employees. However, incentives have an equally valid role to play in ensuring that your organisation can attract and retain people of the right calibre.

It should never be forgotten that businesses compete for high quality staff in much the same way as they do for customers. The same attention has therefore to be paid to competitive strength. The decision to stay or join a competitor is a personal one, but the factors influencing the decision need examination.

These factors can be split down into four constituent elements. There can be incentives for both staying and leaving and similarly there can be deterrents. Broadly, these can be analysed as in Figure 3.

	Incentives	**Frustrations**
To stay	Existing prospects	Frustrations
To leave	Alternative prospects	Handcuffs

Figure 3   Incentives and deterrents

Relative prospects with the existing and new organisations can be analysed by the employee who may, at the end of the day, make his decision based solely on these factors. However, the employee can be deterred from even looking in the market-place for a new job if his 'frustrations' are minimised and his 'handcuffs' maximised. The level of frustration endured by an employee is subjective and hence impossible to quantify. But some of the contributory factors will include:

- Frustrated ambition
- Neglect – being taken for granted
- Feeling unfairly treated
- Poor working conditions
- Unfriendly atmosphere.

The remainder of this chapter will consider the possibilities open to the employer in using golden hellos, handcuffs, and handshakes to attract and retain high quality employees, together with the taxation implications of these courses of action. Share options are by far the most widespread form of golden handcuffs used in the United Kingdom today. They are however governed by special tax rules and for this reason are considered separately in Chapters 8 to 10 of this book.

General background

The success or failure of a business is increasingly dependent on attracting and keeping the right people and getting rid of the wrong ones. Companies are sometimes prepared to make payments to potential key employees to attract them from another company. Similarly, companies often take the view that a suitable payment to a departing key employee can maintain goodwill.

In addition, employment contracts themselves are now being used as a means of attracting the right people and getting rid of the wrong ones. For example, a company may offer a long-term employment contract to a key individual which will enable him to sue for damages if his employment is terminated early (a so-called 'golden parachute'). The contract may also provide penalties for someone who leaves the company before a specified period ('golden handcuffs').

Such payments are not restricted to the highly-paid. Redundancy payments, whether statutory or voluntary, are also common when a company is shedding staff.

It is clear, therefore, that a broad knowledge of the tax rules regarding termination payments and inducement payments is valuable. If correctly structured from a tax point of view, these can enable a company to beat its competitors in attracting key personnel, and obtain a tax deduction for doing so. In some cases it may be possible to make a payment which is completely tax-free in the hands of the recipient. The circumstances are however rather limited and by no means as widespread as the rumours about large tax-free 'golden hellos' to key executives would have us believe.

Tax generally

On first principles, a leaving or joining payment can only be taxable if it falls within one of the various Schedules and Cases under which income tax is charged or, alternatively, if it comes within the ambit of capital gains tax.

The most likely charge is that of Schedule E. This taxes 'emoluments' and is defined to include all 'salaries, fees, wages, and profits whatsoever'. Note that to be taxable these emoluments must come *from* the employment. Clearly, payments which do not stem from the employment contract eg a gift, are not taxable under the general principles of Schedule E.

Special rules for lump sum payments

It is accepted by the tax law that some payments on arrival or departure do not fall within Schedule E. For example, payments of compensation for loss of office cannot be taxed under Schedule E because they are not for services rendered but in settlement of a legal claim the employee may have against his former employer.

Similarly, *ex gratia* payments are by definition not for services rendered but are gifts. The services rendered are remunerated by a market rate salary.

That is not to say that all *ex gratia* or compensation payments will be tax free. There are special golden handshake rules under which, broadly speaking , the first £30,000 of any such payment is tax free, with the excess being taxable in full. This is considered further below.

Golden hellos

How then can an employer pay a tax-free 'golden hello' to a prospective employee? The answer is, 'With difficulty'!

The basic principle is that a 'golden hello' will be held to be taxable if the Inland Revenue can demonstrate that it derives from the employment contract.

Four main principles can be stated:

1. Payments by employers to employees are prima facie taxable emoluments, unless:
   (a) the payments are for full consideration other than services rendered (eg for the purchase of an asset from the employee); or

(b) they amount to a gift in the employee's personal capacity. (This represents the Inland Revenue view, although it has been disputed in a number of cases.)
2. The mere fact that the recipient is an employee does not of itself make the payment an emolument.
3. The fact that the payments are *capital* does not remove them from the *income* tax net. There is no concept of a capital/revenue split in Schedule E taxation.
4. A payment for *giving up an advantages*, rather than a *reward for services*, is probably outside Schedule E (eg an amateur footballer turning professional, a barrister becoming an employed legal adviser). Thus, persons irrevocably relinquishing a profession, eg partners in a firm of stockbrokers, and taking up employment *might* be within this principle.

The main tax planning points on 'golden hellos' are as follows. First, the payment must be *irrevocable*. Thus to achieve non-taxability, the payer must be prepared to take the risk of making the payment without any enforceable right to insist that the induced employee will come. There must be no legally binding commitment to transfer on the part of the recipient of the payment. In addition, the payment should preferably be in exchange for giving up some form of personal benefit, permanently. If this cannot be achieved, it probably has to be accepted that the payment is in the nature of an inducement,and professional advice should be taken.

It must also be demonstrably the case that the payment is not for any services rendered either in the past or in the future. It is essential that the employee can demonstrate that he will be paid the full market rate for the new job. There should be no reduction of the employee's salary on account of the golden hello. For this reason, the fullest possible legal documentation should evidence the inducement payment.

Golden handcuffs

'Golden handcuffs' is a very loose term which is applied to any arrangement giving employees an incentive not to leave their present employer.

One example is the purchase of a business on deferred terms, under which the deferred purchase price, often in the form of shares in the acquiring company, is reduced if the individual leaves his new employer within, say, 5 years. It will not affect the capital gains tax treatment given to the disposal of his goodwill, merely the quantum he receives for it.

But by far the most common form of golden handcuffs is an Inland Revenue Approved Share Option Scheme under which an employee leaving forfeits his share options (see Chapter 9).

In practice, the most effective golden handcuff for employees aged 40 or over is probably membership of a well-run non-contributory final salary occupational pension scheme (see Chapter 6).

AN ARRANGEMENT GIVING EMPLOYEES AN
INCENTIVE NOT TO LEAVE....

Golden handshakes

As has been stated above, the general rule is that the first £30,000 of any termination payment is tax free. The wording of the legislation is extremely wide and brings within its scope all termination payments, whether compensation for loss of office or *ex gratia*.

It should be noted that the special golden handshake rules do not apply where the payment is chargeable to income tax under the general rules of Schedule E. Thus accrued holiday pay remains fully taxable even though it will often be 'buried' as part of the termination package.

On the other hand, a payment in lieu of notice does not derive from the employment (but from the termination of that employment). Hence it is not taxable under the general rules of Schedule E and falls within the 'golden handshake' provisions.

Certain termination payment, are absolutely exempt from the 'golden handshake 'provisions in the tax legislation and hence fall to be totally tax-free. These are:

1. Payments on termination of an employment due to death, injury, or disability (the Inland Revenue Statement of Practice says that 'disability' includes both sudden disability and also disability as a result of a general running-down of faculties).
2. Damages for personal injury.
3. Normal lump sum payments from an approved occupational pension scheme.

Practical aspects

There is no requirement to deduct PAYE from the first £30,000 of a qualifying termination payment.

The excess over £30,000 is subject to PAYE in full if it is paid prior to the employee's departure. If it is paid after the employee has been given his form P45, then only basic rate tax (currently 25%) needs to be deducted.

It is for the employee to claim his own tax relief on the *ex gratia* payment. In many cases the PAYE inspector for the company may allow interim relief via the PAYE coding notice. It is important that the employee files his income tax return as soon as possible after April 5th in the year of assessment in which the *ex gratia* payment is made.

The company making the termination payment must inform its Inspector of Taxes within 30 days of the end of the tax year of the payment, and to whom it was made.

There is no legal obligation on the employee to declare the non-taxable part of the *ex gratia* payment on his tax return but it would not be advisable not to do so.

In arriving at the £30,000 figure, account must be taken of all aspects of the termination payment including, for example, the value of any car or other asset included in the termination package.

Redundancy payments

Statutory redundancy payments payable under the Government's Statutory Redundancy Scheme are not taxable under general Schedule E principles, but are taxable under the 'golden handshake' provisions. Such payments are normally very small, say £2–3,000, but they do count towards the general £30,000 limit.

Non-statutory redundancy payments out of a special redundancy scheme set up by the company and to which the employee has a contractual right are strictly fully taxable under Schedule E. By concession (Inland Revenue Statement of Practice 1/81), the Inland Revenue do not tax such payments except under the golden handshake legislation, and since the first £30,000 of such payments are tax free, no tax normally results.

National Insurance

National Insurance contributions are not payable on termination payments unless, unusually, they arise directly under the employment contract.

Restrictive covenants

A capital payment made to a past employee in respect of an undertaking by him not to compete is fully taxable in the hands of the recipient but tax deductible in the books of the payer.

Quick summary

The following is a quick summary of the more important aspects of golden hellos, handcuffs and handshakes:

- Incentives have a valid role to play in attracting and retaining employees of the right calibre.
- Golden hellos will normally be taxable, although with care 'tax-free' golden hellos can be structured.
- Share option schemes and pension schemes can be an effective golden handcuff.
- In general, the first £30,000 of a golden handshake will be tax free.
- The £30,000 exemption does *not* apply where there is a contractual entitlement to the income. This would include accrued holiday pay but would not include payment in lieu of notice.

Chapter 4

Company Cars

The role of the car in incentive planning

It was stated in Chapter 1 that incentives can be used either:

- to attract and retain people of the right calibre; or
- to elicit a high standard of performance from them.

Although perks and fringe benefits are used in an indirect way to motivate employees to perform (for example where different types of car are offered to different grades of employee), the primary role of any fringe benefit is to enable the organisation to attract and keep the right staff.

The question of visibility has already been considered in the context of non-cash incentives. Visibility is possibly of even greater importance when considering benefits-in-kind and this factor is one of the main reasons for the enduring success of the company car as a perk, notwithstanding the very substantial increases in the taxation of company cars in recent years.

Other fringe benefits, notably pensions (see Chapter 6) and share options (see Chapters 8 to 10), can be an important constituent of the remuneration package and retention of staff. But none carries the same degree of emotive response as the company car.

The employee's position

It is often said that a car is the second most expensive asset acquired by an individual, second only to buying a home. However, in corporate Britain today only a minority of executives actually own the car they drive. Historically this has been due to the tax effectiveness of the car as well as the perceived status of driving a new car.

As a result the company car is one of the most widespread and certainly the most visible of all fringe benefits. Indeed it has been said that there is probably only one other country in the world apart from Britain where the car a person drives so accurately reflects his position in the corporate hierarchy: the Soviet Union! In Britain the car is often seen as a status symbol – if you drive a Jaguar you are almost certainly a chairman or managing director; a Mercedes suggests you are on the Board; a Ford Escort or Sierra, and you hold a far more lowly position.

The car is of course a uniquely visible fringe benefit and status symbol. At home, the sight of the company car sitting in your driveway probably says more about your level of income than you would ever otherwise admit to neighbours and passers-by. Similarly colleagues at work who would never dream of asking how much you earn will have no such qualms when asking about the car you drive.

THE SIGHT OF THE **COMPANY CAR** SITTING ON YOUR DRIVE PROBABLY SAYS **MORE ABOUT YOUR LEVEL OF INCOME** THAN YOU WOULD EVER ADMIT....

The taxation of company cars has been a favourite subject of successive Chancellors for many years. In recent years cars have been the subject of considerable political attention for reasons best summarised in the consultative paper on the 'Taxation of Cars and Petrol as Benefits in Kind' issued by the Inland Revenue in August 1979, which stated:

'It is recognised that, in a regime of very high personal tax rates, there will inevitably be a tendency towards remuneration in the form of non-pecuniary benefits rather than in the form of cash. ... Since car benefits are believed to account for about eighty per cent of the total value of fringe benefits (apart from pension provisions) the Government considers it appropriate to begin with a review of that sector.'

Although the top rate of tax was reduced from 83% to 60% in 1979 and from 60% to 40% in 1988 it is clear that cars are still a favourite area for political attention. Indeed the taxable value on which company car users are taxed (the scale benefit) tripled between 1988 and 1990.

Any director or employee earning over £8,500 per annum who has the private use of a car will be assessed to income tax by reference to a 'scale benefit'. The scale benefit is determined by reference to the age, cost, and cylinder capacity of the car. The scale benefit does not however apply to employees who are neither directors nor earning at a rate in excess of £8,500 per year.

The car scale benefits for 1990/91 are set out in Table 2.

Table 2 Car scale benefits 1990/91

	Cars aged under 4 years £	Cars Aged over 4 years £
Cars up to £19,250		
Cylinder capacity:		
1400 cc or less	1,700	1,150
1401 to 2000 cc	2,200	1,500
Over 2000 cc	3,550	2,350
Cars over £19,250		
£19,251 to £29,000	4,600	3,100
Over £29,000	7,400	4,900

The car scale benefit is increased by 50% where the car is a 'perk' car, that is, either business mileage is less than 2,500 miles per annum or the car is a second or subsequent car. Conversely, the car scale benefit is halved where the car is used preponderantly for business motoring, that is, where business mileage is in excess of 18,000 miles per year.

The car scale benefit is reduced on a pound for pound basis where the employee is required to make a contribution for the use of the car.

There is a separate scale benefit where petrol or other fuel is provided for private motoring, as shown in Table 3.

Table 3   Fuel scale benefit 1990/91

Cylinder capacity	£
1400 cc or less	480
1401 to 2000 cc	600
Over 2000 cc	900

The fuel scale benefit is reduced by 50% where business mileage is in excess of 18,000 miles per year. It is not, however, increased where business mileage is under 2,500 miles or for second or subsequent cars.

Unlike the car benefit, the fuel scale benefit is an 'all or nothing' charge which cannot be reduced on a pound for pound basis if the employee is required to make a contribution for the use of the car. It is, however, eliminated if the employee is required to bear all the costs of private motoring.

The scale benefits are reduced on a pro rata basis where the car is unavailable for use by the employee or where it is incapable of being used for a consecutive period of thirty days. So a car provided half-way through the tax year would have been unavailable for the first six months and the scale benefit would accordingly be halved. Similarly where a car is incapable of being used for at least thirty consecutive days, for example if it was undergoing repairs at a garage and was thus off the road, the scale benefit would be proportionately reduced. It is understood that the Revenue may also accept a proportionate reduction where an employee who is undertaking an overseas trip returns the car to his employer so that the car is no longer available for his use or for use by other members of his family or household.

Examples

1. Jonathan, a sales representative, is provided with a Ford Sierra 1.6L by his employer. He has substantial business mileage (over 18,000 miles per annum). He is not allowed private petrol.

   The appropriate car scale benefit of £2,200 is reduced by 50% because the car is used preponderantly for business motoring. As a result, Jonathan will pay tax on £1100, which at the basic rate of tax (25%) amounts to £275.

2. Emma, a company director, is provided with a prestige car costing £25,000. She has little business mileage and all petrol is paid for by her company.

   The appropriate scale benefits are £4,600 for the car and £900 (assuming the cylinder capacity is over 2 litre) in respect of the private petrol. Because business mileage is below 2,500 miles per annum, the car scale benefit is increased by 50%. The fuel scale benefit is not, however, increased. As a result, Emma will pay tax on £7,800, which at her highest marginal rate of 40% amounts to £3,120.

It should be noted that where there has been an element of 'salary sacrifice', the employee may be taxed under the general charging provisions of Schedule E rather than the specific rules applying to company cars. Salary sacrifice may include arrangements where the employee accepts reduced salary in return for a car or where he is entitled to surrender his company car in favour of an increase in salary.

No benefit is deemed to arise on the use of a company car provided the car is part of a 'pool'. However, the requirements to be satisfied are stringent and are strictly interpreted by the Inland Revenue. A car qualifies as a pool car only if all the following conditions are satisfied:

(a) It is available for, and used by, more than one employee and is not ordinarily used by any one of them to the exclusion of the others.
(b) Any private use of the car is merely incidental to its business use.
(c) It is not normally kept overnight at or near the residence of any of the employees unless it is kept on the employer's premises.

Car parking and car telephones

Perhaps ironically in view of the hefty increases in car scale benefits over the past few years, the Inland Revenue have introduced new reliefs in respect of car parking and car telephones.

For many years, the Inland Revenue view was that the provision of car parking was a benefit-in-kind separately assessable from the provision of the car itself. However, following numerous disputes with tax practitioners over invariably small amounts of tax, they backed down on this question and legislation was introduced in the Finance Act 1988 to bring within the ambit of the car scale benefit the provision of a car parking space at or near the place of work.

As a result the provision of car parking (such as at a local garage) for company car users is now a tax-free perk.

On a similar issue, many Inland Revenue inspectors sought in the past to assess the provision of a car telephone as a separate benefit outside the normal car scale charge. As with car parking, the argument was that car telephones are a cost of the driver and not a cost of the car.

The Inland Revenue subsequently backed down and conceded in a Statement of Practice (5/88 dated 22 July 1988) that no assessable benefit in respect of either calls or rental will arise provided the telephone cannot be used separately from the car. By inference, an assessable benefit may arise in respect of *portable* car telephones. A benefit may also arise if telephones are fitted in cars owned privately by employees.

Thus, it would now appear that car telephones are a perk that can be provided to selected employees without any additional tax liability arising.

The choice of car

The choice of car offered to an employee or director is normally restricted by his employer by reference to one of the following:

- A specific make or model
- The capital cost or value
- The monthly cost.

A restriction by reference to a benchmark car is a common choice as it allows the restriction to increase automatically with car price inflation. It may however mean that employees are unnecessarily restricted as to choice of car and this may cause some degree of resentment.

An alternative is to allow employees to select their car by reference to its capital cost or value. Although this does allow employees far greater choice in selecting the car it can give rise to problems for the employer. There can be a wide discrepancy between the running costs of cars with similar capital values (due to factors such as insurance group, cost of spare parts, petrol consumption, depreciation, etc). For this reason, employers will often seek to restrict the choice of cars within the capital cost limit, for example to British or EC cars.

The third method of restricting employee choice (that is, by reference to monthly cost) is possibly the fairest as between employee and employer. The employee is allowed a wide choice of car but the employer is protected from the vagaries of running costs. The practical problem is one of establishing the monthly costs of different cars although this solution can be overcome by contract hiring the car.

The employer's position

From the employer's point of view, the acquisition and maintenance of a fleet of company cars can be a considerable financial and administrative burden.

How the car fleet is acquired will be determined by factors such as cashflow requirements, size of fleet, the need to control costs, and personal preferences. The tax implications of the alternative methods of acquisition should not be ignored.

Paying cash is still the most popular method of buying vehicles – either out of existing funds or from bank borrowings. No deduction is allowed in computing profits for tax purposes for the cost of the car or for the annual depreciation charge. Instead, 25% writing-down allowances are given on the total cost of the car.

The VAT suffered on the purchase of the car is not an allowable input but can be added to the cost on which writing-down allowances are claimed.

Cars costing less than £8,000 are pooled for tax purposes. Writing-down allowances are given on the balance of the pool after including additions and deducting disposals. More expensive cars must be separately identified. There is an overall restriction on the annual writing-down allowance of £2,000 per car.

If the car is purchased with a bank loan or overdraft, the interest will normally be allowable as a trading deduction.

For capital gains tax purposes the car is an exempt asset and accordingly neither capital gain nor allowable loss will arise on its disposal.

The tax treatment of acquiring a car by way of hire or lease purchase is exactly the same as that of cash purchase. The car is treated as having been acquired on the date the contract was entered into rather than the date on which the purchase option is exercised and legal title passed. As with cash purchases, writing-down allowances will be available on the capital cost of the car and the interest element of the HP instalments may be treated as a trading deduction.

Before the passing of the Finance Act 1980, car leasing had been extremely attractive and had gained something of a mystique as a tax-saving panacea. Lessors were entitled to 100% first-year allowances, rather than the normal 25% writing-down allowances on cars. The benefits were in turn passed on to the lessee by way of reduced lease rentals.

However, the Finance Act 1980 denied first-year allowances to lessors and reduced the allowances to 25% writing-down allowances. As a result, the tax incentive to leasing cars has now disappeared. Nonetheless, some companies may still see car leasing as convenient or profitable on other grounds.

For the company using the car, the lease rentals are fully tax-deductible provided the price tag on the car when new is less than £8,000. Above the £8,000 retail price, a percentage of the lease rentals will be disallowed for tax purposes (see Table 4).

Table 4 Percentage of lease rentals allowable as tax deductions

Retail price when new £	% Rental allowance
8,000	100.00
9,000	94.44
10,000	90.00
11,000	86.36
12,000	83.33
13,000	80.77
14,000	78.57
15,000	76.67
16,000	75.00
17,000	73.53
18,000	72.22
19,000	71.05
20,000	70.00
21,000	69.05
22,000	68.18
23,000	67.39
24,000	66.67
25,000	66.00
26,000	65.38
27,000	64.81
28,000	64.29
29,000	63.79
30,000	63.33

The allowable percentage of the lease rental is calculated as the proportion that £8,000, plus one-half of the difference between £8,000 and the retail price when new, bears to the actual retail price of the car.

Where R is the new retail price, this formula can be expressed as:

$$1 - \frac{(R - £8,000)}{2R}$$

As a result, for a car costing £10,000, only 90% of the lease rental will be deductible for tax purposes, and for a £16,000 car only 75% of the lease rental will be tax-deductible.

The lease rental restriction is slightly similar to the restriction on writing-down allowances on the purchase of expensive cars. But the restriction on writing-down allowances is only a deferment of the allowances whereas the lease rental restriction is a permanent disallowance. In addition, the lessor of a more expensive car will have suffered a restriction on writing-down allowances which he or she will no doubt seek to pass on to the lessee by way of increased rentals. It is therefore likely that the lessee of a more expensive car will effectively suffer a double restriction.

The Inland Revenue have announced that where a lessee receives a refund of rentals in respect of the lease of an expensive car, a percentage of the refund may be treated as non-taxable in the same way as the earlier payments were restricted by the leasing formula for expensive cars.

VAT on car purchase is not an allowable input for VAT purposes, but the VAT charged on lease rentals is an allowable input. At first sight this might appear to represent a significant advantage of leasing over purchase. But the lessor will have suffered irrevocable VAT on the purchase and that will no doubt be passed on to the lessee by way of increased lease rentals.

Contract hire v. finance leasing

Contract hire and finance leasing are both types of leasing arrangements. With a finance lease, the owner or lessor provides the car in return for a rental but takes no responsibility for maintenance. The lessee accepts all the risks and rewards of ownership.

With contract hire, the owner or lessor accepts the risks and rewards of ownership. Thus, the lessee would pay a rental for the car while the lessor would be responsible for all repairs and maintenance of the car. In most cases the lessor will also provide a relief vehicle service if the car spends time off the road.

For tax purposes contract hire and finance leasing are both treated as car leasing and are subject to the tax rules previously explained.

However, the percentage restriction on leasing cars costing more than £8,000 is applied to the rental paid for the use of the car. So a lessee under a contract hire arrangement must ensure that the repairs and maintenance element of the rental is covered by a separate contract. Otherwise, it will be subject to the percentage restriction as well.

You will not want the tax tail to wag the commercial dog, but tax considerations should not be overlooked. In particular, leasing expensive cars carries a tax penalty which can be avoided if cars are purchased or hire-purchased.

Buying a car will give rise to capital allowances, but these will be of little use if the company is not in a tax-paying position. It may be better to lease the car and effectively sell the allowances to the lessor.

Quick summary

- Cars are the most visible and emotive of all fringe benefits. This is one of the main reasons for the enduring success of the company car as a perk, notwithstanding the substantial tax increases in recent years.
- Employees are taxed by reference to a scale charge which has tripled in just three years.
- From the employer's point of view, running a car fleet can be a considerable financial and administrative burden.
- Leasing expensive cars carries a tax penalty which can be avoided if cars are purchased or hire-purchased.

Chapter 5

Other Fringe Benefits

General

The number of alternative fringe benefits offered to employees need only be limited by the imagination of the employer. For example, some employers operate a 'cafeteria' system whereby employees can select their own benefits package from the wide range on offer. Colloquially, this is also known as the 'shopping basket' or, even more colourfully, the 'grab bag' approach to remuneration planning.

This chapter discusses in outline some of the more common fringe benefits offered by employers. Few employers will want to offer all the benefits described in this chapter (if only because of the administrative repercussions) but most employers will find several that are of interest to their own organisations.

Cafeteria benefits

The essence of a cafeteria system of flexible employee benefits is that the perceived attraction of different benefits will vary from employee to employee. For example, there are a growing number of families with two company cars where both husband and wife are working. In many cases, one partner might be glad of the opportunity to hand back the keys of his or her car in order to receive an alternative benefit of, say, company-subsidised childcare.

Similarly, an employee in his twenties might be more motivated by a higher–specification company car than by an increased pension. The reverse might be true of an employee in his fifties.

The cafeteria benefits system is widespread in the United States but far less common in the United Kingdom. This position is likely to change over the next few years as competition for skilled labour becomes more intense.

A cafeteria benefits system would probably operate by allocating each eligible employee a certain number of benefit points which could then be 'spent' as the employee chooses on a range of company–offered benefits. Core benefits – that is, those benefits that the employer considers must be offered – will be compulsory. Other benefits can be either encouraged or discouraged by the allocation of a high or low points 'price' for each benefit.

Core benefits would normally include a certain number of days' holiday, pension provision and life cover. However, the core benefits could be increased out of the employee's points allocation if he so wishes.

The unpopularity of cafeteria benefits in the UK to date has been largely due to a suspicion that the administrative cost would outweigh the attractions of flexible benefits. However, with the advent of appropriate computer software packages, this is unlikely to be a major problem for much longer.

Use of company assets

The Inland Revenue assess as an annual benefit the use of company assets by directors and higher paid employees. Assets which may be involved include yachts, furniture, television sets, stereo equipment, and clothing.

The annual value on which the employee is assessed is 20% of the asset's market value at the date it was first made available for use by the employee.

Notwithstanding the above, many companies find it attractive to provide key employees with the use of assets. In particular, schemes have been set up by retailers (for example Austin Reed) under which the employer purchases clothing for its directors and employees. Under such a scheme, the employer buys, for example, a suit costing £200. The employee will pay tax on a benefit of £40 (20% × £200) for each year in which the suit is available for his use. If the suit is no longer required after, say, three years no further tax charge will arise on the employee.

Although the position is not free from doubt, it is likely that the clothing will be deductible for the employer either as a revenue expense or as an asset on which writing-down allowances may be claimed.

It is important that the goods are purchased, and seen to be purchased, by the company. Accordingly, account cards in the name of individual employees should be avoided.

If an asset which has been provided for the use of an employee is subsequently transferred to him tax will be payable on the difference between the cost of the asset (or market value at the date of transfer if higher) less the amounts charged to tax on the employee and the amount paid by the employee for the asset.

Luncheon facilities

Meals provided free of charge or at low cost in a canteen on the firm's premises are not taxable if they are available to staff generally. Furthermore, the use of a separate room by directors and senior staff does not prejudice this exemption.

The Inland Revenue published an extra-statutory concession in January 1990 which widens the scope for employers providing free or subsidised meals for employees. Employees will not be taxable provided the meals are provided on a reasonable scale, and either:

- all employees are entitled to free or subsidised meals on the employer's premises or elsewhere; or
- the employer provides free or subsidised meal vouchers for staff for whom meals are not provided.

This new concession extends considerably the possibilities open to employers. In particular, it appears that the use of exclusive dining facilities by senior staff will no longer be a taxable benefit, provided other employees are given meal vouchers of a modest amount. The irony is that although the executives would not be taxed on the use of the dining facility, the employees would be taxed on the provision of meal vouchers to the extent that they exceed 15 pence per day (see below).

THE USE OF A **SEPARATE ROOM BY DIRECTORS** DOES NOT PREJUDICE THIS EXEMPTION....

Luncheon vouchers offer an alternative to the provision of canteen facilities. However, exemption from income tax in respect of these vouchers is strictly controlled and certain criteria must be complied with: the vouchers must be non-transferable and not capable of being exchanged for cash. Furthermore, the maximum tax-free limit is only 15p per working day.

Medical insurance

The payment of an employee's medical insurance in respect of schemes run by BUPA, PPP, and similar organisations is a deductible expense for the purposes of corporation tax. The majority of such schemes also covers the employee's immediate family.

The employee will be assessed to tax on a benefit-in-kind in respect of the premiums paid by the employer. Despite this, payment of medical insurance is still an attractive perk since the employer will generally be in a position to negotiate a lower premium rate than the individual. In addition, National Insurance contributions are not payable on the benefit.

From April 1990, tax relief for health insurance will be available to the over-60s.

Cheap loans

Where a lower-paid employee receives an interest-free or low interest loan, no taxable benefit arises. A charge will, however, generally arise in respect of loans made to directors and higher-paid employees. The assessable benefit is calculated as the difference between the amount of interest actually paid, if any, and interest at the 'official rate'. The official rate is adjusted on a regular basis in line with market rates, but is currently $16^{1}/_{2}\%$.

No benefit is deemed to arise if the loan has been obtained for a qualifying purpose, for example:

- Loans up to £30,000 to purchase a main residence
- Loans to acquire shares in, or for making a loan to, a close company in which the individual has a 'material' interest (broadly speaking, 5% together with his associates).
- Loans to acquire a share in, or for making a loan to, a partnership of which the individual is a partner.

It should not be overlooked that most loans over £2,500 to company directors are prohibited under the Companies Act.

No assessment is made provided that notional interest at the 'official rate' is less than £200. In effect this means that an interest-free loan of approximately £2,500 may be made without any tax liability for the employee, provided the loan is repaid by monthly instalments over the course of the year. This would normally cover season ticket loans.

A liability to tax will arise if the loan is released or written-off. The liability, based on the amount thus released or written off,will arise regardless of whether or not the person concerned is still employed by that company. These provisions will not be enacted where the loan is forgiven upon the death of the employee.

Accommodation

It is possible for employees to be provided with accommodation which is either rented or owned by the employer. However, the provision of accommodation is a taxable benefit, the extent of which is dependent on whether the property is rented or owned by the employer. These rules apply to all employees and not just directors and the higher paid.

In the case of rented property, the assessable benefit-in-kind is the rent paid by the employer less any contribution made by the employee.

Where the employer owns the property, the assessable amount is the 'annual value'of the property for rating purposes. This is likely to be substantially below the real value to the employee of occupying the property.

An additional charge may arise where the employer paid more than £75,000 to acquire the property. The amount by which the cost exceeds £75,000 is treated as a beneficial loan (see above) and an assessment is made accordingly.

Where the accommodation is provided together with furniture and fittings, an additional charge will arise of 20% of the cost of the furniture and fittings.

Some employers purchase holiday flats or cottages for use by staff. Strictly speaking, each member of staff could be assessed on the full amount of the gross annual value of the property in line with the provisions outlined above. In practice however, the Inland Revenue apportion the assessable amount for the year amongst the employees who have occupied the property.

No charge to tax will arise, however, if it is necessary or customary for the accommodation to be provided, or if there is a special threat to security.

Tax-free relocation

Where an employee is required to move home in order to take up a new post, certain costs can be reimbursed by the employer without any income tax charge arising:

- the net cost (after tax relief) of any bridging finance taken out on the old property, provided certain conditions are met;
- any loss suffered on the old property because a quick sale was necessary;
- if the employee was required to move to a more expensive area, the reimbursement of any additional annual costs are tax free for a number of years;
- legal and professional fees, removal costs and insurance;
- travel and hotel costs while looking for a new property and at the time of the move;
- a subsistence allowance to cover any period while the employee is waiting to move into his new home; and
- a disturbance allowance (of perhaps 10% or 12.5% of salary) to cover connection charges, replacement of curtains, carpets, school uniforms, etc.

Telephone allowances

Where an employer meets the cost in whole or in part of his employee's telephone bill, the payments made will rank as a benefit on the employee. However, to the extent the employee can justify that the telephone was used for business purposes, a claim may be made for the assessable benefit arising in connection with the telephone bill (including in certain limited cases the telephone rental) to be reduced proportionately.

Suggestion schemes

In order to generate cost savings, many employers operate staff suggestion schemes which encourage employees to put forward ideas for improving their firm's efficiency or productivity. Successful ideas are recognised by a cash payment. By concession, the Inland Revenue do not tax such payments provided the scheme meets certain conditions, the main ones being that

(a) the scheme is formally constituted and open to all employed on equal terms.
(b) the suggestions fall outside the employee's normal duties.
(c) for payments over £25 the suggestion must have been accepted for implementation, and

(d) the awards made must be calculated by reference to specified fractions of the expected financial benefit to the business, with an overriding tax limit of £5,000.

It would be unwise to rely on this concession to make a payment to a director, and where significant sums are involved it would be advisable to agree the position with the Inland Revenue in advance.
   The full text of the concession is reproduced in Appendix 2.

Long-service awards

It has become customary in certain companies to make awards to directors and employees in recognition of their loyalty and long service. Provided that the period of service is at least 20 years, and no similar award has been made to the employee within the previous 10 years, the gift will by Inland Revenue concession be exempt from income tax. The gift must not be in cash and may not exceed £20 in value for each year of service. The gift may take the form of tangible articles (for example, a gold watch) or of shares in the employing company (or another company in the same group).

Sporting facilities

The Inland Revenue will not normally seek to tax the modest provision of sporting facilities, whether on the company's premises or where the firm takes out a corporate membership with an outside club, provided this is for the benefit of employees generally.
   Tax may, however, be charged if the cost per employee is substantial or if the employer takes out a subscription for only a small group of employees and directors.

Nursery facilities

Following intense pressure on the Government to announce concessionary or legislative tax relief from the taxation as a benefit-in-kind of nursery or crèche facilities, a limited relief was finally announced in the 1990 Budget.
   The political controversy was first highlighted in a Parliamentary Question and Answer in April 1985, when the then Financial Secretary to the Treasury, Mr John Moore MP, contradicted the widely held understanding that subsidised nursery facilities were by concession not taxable. This misunderstanding by the tax-paying public generally had been fuelled by advice to that effect given in both the Equal Opportunities Commission manual and the *Which? Tax Saving Guide.*

In these exceptional circumstances, the Inland Revenue agreed not to seek to recover back tax where nursery facilities had been provided for periods prior to 6 April 1985. They confirmed, however, that the provision of such facilities was in law fully taxable on the recipients (other than employees earning at a rate less than £8,500 per annum).

The new relief, which was introduced with effect from 6 April 1990, provides that employer–provided childcare facilities are now exempt from tax as an employee benefit. It does not matter if the nursery or crèche is located at the workplace or elsewhere (although domestic premises are specifically excluded).

It is a condition of the exemption that the childcare facilities should comply with any legal requirement for registration by the local authority. But it is possible for one or more employers (together with voluntary organisations or local authorities, perhaps) to run a nursery jointly and for their employees still to enjoy the tax relief. Unfortunately, the new tax exemption does not apply where the employee is paid an allowance, or given a childcare voucher, which he or she can then use to pay directly to a third party. By excluding childcare vouchers, the Government has not completely removed the tax disincentive to women returning to work after having children.

Employers often draw their workforce from a wide geographical area and as a result, any nursery they might provide would need to be at a central location, probably at or near the workplace. The costs of providing nurseries are, therefore, likely to be high (particularly in major population centres such as London) and hence, unattractive to the majority of employers.

In addition, the parent will have to incur additional transportation costs bringing the children to the nursery. The prospect of large numbers of 'toddler commuters' being taken on to rush–hour trains and buses is surely unlikely.

If childcare vouchers had also been exempted, parents could have used nurseries local to their homes in preference to turning their children into commuters. Notwithstanding the lack of tax relief for childcare vouchers, it is anticipated that this alternative method of providing nursery facilities as an employee benefit will become increasingly popular with employers and employees alike.

Quick summary

A list of the more common fringe benefits is set out below.

- Use of company assets (eg, yachts, furniture, television sets, stereo equipment and clothing)
- Canteens and luncheon vouchers
- Medical insurance
- Company accommodation
- Tax-free relocation
- Telephone allowances
- Suggestion schemes
- Long-service awards
- Sporting facilities
- Crèches and nursery facilities.

Chapter 6

The Role of Pensions in Incentive Planning

General

Although pensions are by far the most widespread of all fringe benefits (half of all directors and employees belong to a company pension scheme), they are also one of the least visible. It is a sad fact that most employees show a distinct lack of interest when faced with the question of pension planning.

That position is however altering rapidly. The Government have in recent years made fundamental and wide-ranging changes to the pension regime as a result of which more and more employees are becoming pension-aware.

Although most of the modifications have been made to assist job mobility, higher paid employees may become more reluctant to move as a result of one of the changes introduced by the Finance Act 1989. The effect of this was to limit to £60,000 the maximum salary upon which tax-efficient pensions could be based and funded. These provisions do not apply to members of existing pension schemes but will immediately have effect when an employee changes job and in so doing leaves one pension scheme and joins another.

Although the £60,000 limit will maintain its real value over the years by being increased in line with the Retail Prices Index (and after one year's indexation is now £64,800), it will not keep its value in salary inflation terms, which has tended to grow 2% per annum faster than price inflation. In 20 years' time the equivalent threshold salary will be £40,000 in today's terms, which will bring an ever-increasing section of the workforce into the capping limitation, and will apply to far more than the Government-indicated 3% of the working population.

The effect may be to discourage younger, high earners from frequent moves. Or it may make them more aware of pensions since these new restrictions will make it more difficult to fund aggressively for an adequate pension later in life. Companies seeking to attract senior employees from rival organisations may therefore need to compensate the new employee for the pension costs of moving by revising their current remuneration options. Many of the possible non-pension solutions to overcome this brake on mobility will be found elsewhere in this book. In particular, it is envisaged that share option schemes (see Chapters 8 to 10) will become increasingly popular.

In reviewing the pension scheme as a part of the incentive package to be offered to an individual the company will need to be aware of the pension 'status' of that individual. Prior to 17 March 1987 the Inland Revenue rules for maximum benefits were:

1. Retirement could be taken from 60 onwards (55 for females).
2. A full 2/3rds pension could be taken after 10 years' service.
3. A lump sum of 1.5 times salary could be taken after 20 years' service (this would reduce the income available).
4. For those dying in service before retirement, a tax-free lump sum of 4 times salary could be paid, along with a pension to spouse of 4/9ths of salary, with additional income to financial dependents.
5. Any pension paid could be increased in line with inflation.

Individuals joining a pension scheme after 17 March 1987 and before 14 March 1989 found that:

1. an absolute maximum had been imposed on the salary level that could be used in calculating the lump sum at retirement, which was, and has remained at, £100,000, and
2. the maximum pension could only be obtained after 20 years' service.

In 1989 individuals joining a new scheme after 14 March, or an established scheme on or after 1 June, found that:

1. the maximum salary level used for lump sum and now also pension calculations had been reduced to £60,000, but
2. a full pension could be taken from age 50, and
3. the £60,000 would be increased each year in line with the rate of Price Inflation. (The indexed figure currently stands at £64,800.)

It is obvious that an executive earning £200,000 a year is significantly affected by the changes in the event of a job move, which may allow his current company to use pension planning quite positively in any retention and incentive package. There will, however, be other employees who would be more attracted to the early retirement facilities, or as explained later, could profit from having their own personal pension scheme.

The decline in the birth rate in the 1960s and 1970s will create a distinct shortage of quality personnel in the 1990s so that incentive planning will be important. The changes in pension legislation that have occurred are a strange amalgam of increased flexibility and restrictions, so that designing a scheme or combination of schemes to fit in with future trends will require a better knowledge of the make-up of a company's workforce, including age, salary, and service structure, than is generally available at the present time. While pensions will have a large part to play in incentive planning it will be necessary to ensure provisions meet the real needs of the workforce, and that they are perceived to be relevant.

Final salary schemes

Final salary schemes are the most traditional form of corporate pension planning for the larger company. They operate on the basis of providing a specific level of benefits at retirement, based on a percentage of earnings for each year of service. For example, a scheme may provide as a pension 1/60th of final salary for each year of service. Thus, if an employee has completed 30 years' service at retirement, he can expect 30/60ths, or one half, of his final salary as a pension for life.

Because this scheme is designed to provide specific benefits for a large and ever-changing number of people at retirement, the costing of it is a complicated procedure which requires the services of an actuary to determine the annual contribution necessary to provide those benefits.

This calculation is influenced, amongst other things, by the age structure of the scheme, which will be constantly altered by staff movements. This will affect the amount of benefits required and hence the cost of providing those benefits.

The popularity of final salary schemes in the past, for the company, has stemmed from the cross-subsidy by younger members for the older, and by the poor transfer values that were provided for scheme leavers. As a result the cost of providing long-serving employees with reasonable benefits was kept to a minimum.

While the 1980s have seen the phenomenon of scheme surpluses, and contribution holidays, there has also been a dramatic increase in the level of legislation, litigation, and EC directives which have related to pension schemes, causing significant increases in the required level of funding, without necessarily increasing the benefits for the long-term employee.

A major cause of this increase has related to the provision of realistic transfer values for early leavers. This has come at a time when mobility of labour has increased dramatically, thus imposing significant burdens on final salary schemes, and there are sufficient developments in the pipeline to ensure that funding requirements will increase further.

While the position of the early leaver has been improved, the early retiree can still find himself heavily penalised, because most schemes have a discounting system. For example if, after completing 20 years' service, an employee leaves a 1/60th scheme 5 years before the normal retirement age, there is a double reduction. First the pension will be based on 20/60ths rather than 25/60ths; and second, there will be a discounting process which amounts to just under 5% a year for each year that the individual retires early, so in this case there would be a further reduction of approximately 25%, reducing the pension to 15/60ths of salary. Recent legal and quasi-legal decisions have now brought the legality of this discounting into question, which will be a benefit for the employee, but a further cost for the employer.

The main drawback of final salary schemes is that the employer has no control over the cost of the scheme, and is effectively increasing the benefits for those who leave early, rather than improving the lot of those who remain.

Targeting better benefits for specific individuals is also difficult since they will either have to be defined and disclosed to the general scheme membership, or they can be established on an *ad hoc* basis, using part of the scheme surpluses, though again the information will be available for the main body of scheme membership. The latter approach is made more difficult by the legal requirement to keep the assets of the scheme within 105% of the definable liabilities.

A good quality final salary scheme will act as an excellent morale booster for staff in general, especially if it is well explained and publicised. It is less effective in specifically enhancing the benefits of an individual as part of a more narrowly targeted benefit enhancement package. But there are other options.

Money purchase schemes

As stated above, final salary schemes are driven by the provision of specific benefits. The alternative to this is that the employer can elect to pay a specified monetary contribution for the employee. This may be expressed as a percentage of salary or indeed a particular amount. In this way, the employer remains in control of the cost of the scheme.

A money purchase scheme can be provided for any number of people from one to many thousands. The group pension scheme would be written in such a way that although a group policy is produced, effectively every employee has an identifiable pension fund. This approach provides more flexibility in terms of cost to the employer, and is more readily identifiable to the employee in terms of a benefit, since he would receive an annual statement showing the capital value of his own pension fund, rather than merely being part of a large fund. This method also enables an employer to be flexible in respect of the contribution level for each employee or group of employees. The benefits available at retirement are limited only by reference to the Inland Revenue maxima.

The Occupational Pensions Board have recently relaxed their interpretation of the accrual rate of benefits under a money purchase scheme for transfer purposes so it is possible to cater for increasing levels of funding contribution, which will positively recognise long service. In a final salary scheme the employer contributes proportionately more for the older employee, and a long term server will obtain a proportionately better transfer value than an early leaver, reflecting that service. In a money purchase scheme, however, the tendency has been to provide a single level of input throughout, eg 5% of salary, so there is no recognition of age or service. Transfer values have therefore tended to favour the transient employee against the loyal. The solution is to 'step' the contribution so that, for example, after 5 years' pensionable service there is an increase to 7.5% of salary, and after a further 5 years it again increases to 10%. It is possible to create a general targeting program so that you would aim to provide, say, 50% of salary for an average employee, and design a contribution strategy around that.

Executive 'top hat' schemes

An executive 'top hat' arrangement is the money purchase concept used to target benefits for specific individuals. It can be run as the sole pension arrangement of an individual, or as an additional and parallel arrangement to any group scheme.

The advantage of this arrangement is that the company can direct additional contributions for the benefit of an individual without it being general knowledge through the disclosure regulations that are now an important part of the administrative requirements of a group pension scheme. The overall level of benefit can be adjusted; retirement ages can be brought forward; discounting under the main scheme can be offset for early retirees; and individuals can choose where their funds are invested. These arrangements can often be used in the place of endowments when arranging mortgages.

The executive top hat arrangement is particularly appropriate where pension provision is being made for the top executives, but it is probably not suitable for very large groups. The administration tends to be greater than with other schemes, since every employee will have an individual policy document with individual annual statements.

The small self-administered pension scheme (SSAS) is a specific example of this type of pension, allowing a very high level of personal involvement in the investment of funds. There can be no legal 'earmarking' of investments for specific individuals, so that decisions need to be taken and agreed on a group basis, which in practice means that the membership of the scheme should be small if the result is not to be the proverbial 'camel' in investment performance!

The Inland Revenue will only allow one SSAS per company so membership must be very selective.

Additional voluntary contributions (AVCs)

A group pension arrangement may make the facility of AVCs available to all members of the scheme. As from 26 October 1987, employees have been able to effect 'free-standing' AVCs (FSAVCs) to a company of their choice, so long as they are indeed members of their company scheme. AVCs and FSAVCs enable employees to contribute personally to a separate pension fund which is governed by the same rules as the main pension scheme. Tax relief at the highest marginal rate of income tax is available to employees on any contribution they make, and the maximum they can contribute in any year is 15% of their salary (which would include any ordinary contributions to the main scheme).

The fund produced by AVCs must be used to purchase income only, that is, no cash can be taken. However cash, within Inland Revenue limits, can be taken from the fund created by the ordinary contributions of the employee to the scheme. It can be beneficial, if the scheme rules will allow, for the employee to renegotiate the level of ordinary contribution he makes to the scheme; adjustments to the rate of ordinary contribution may not be made within twelve months of the last adjustment.

Since an AVC facility is a compulsory feature of any company pension scheme, it is normally in the employer's interest to ensure that it is attractive to the scheme members. It is surprising how many schemes consist solely of Building Society accounts, which are, historically, competitive only in the very short term. The Finance Act

1989 has reduced the level of administration that companies have to complete when individuals set up FSAVCs, but it has not been eliminated, and the potential administrative problems are significant, without providing any positive feedback to the company.

While the 15% limit is strictly controlled, it is no longer vital to ensure that the individual is not 'overfunding'. In the past any overfunding by the individual has been to the benefit of the pension scheme because the individuals' fund had to be applied to providing pension benefits. If this reduced the level that the company were able to provide before hitting Inland Revenue limits then the individual suffered. The Finance Act 1989 now allows for a repayment of part of the member's fund, less a tax charge. The level of the tax charge is high, being 35% for a basic rate taxpayer, and 48% for a higher rate payer. This charge is designed to take into account the tax relief enjoyed when the money was invested and the tax-free environment of pension funds.

It does, however, mean that it is unlikely to be beneficial for the individual to over-invest, in which case it would be of value for the scheme to be able to make professional advice available to the member who is likely to be in a position to come up against these limits. This is likely to be a more common occurrence for higher-paid individuals who also have retained benefits under the old pension regimes, but now come under benefit capping.

Salary and bonus sacrifices

As an alternative to AVCs it is possible for the individual to sacrifice part of his entitlement to salary or bonus, so that the company has greater resources to invest into pension arrangements on that individual's behalf. This will tend to occur when either pension provision is low and it is necessary to fund at a higher rate than 15% to make up the deficiency, or there are high bonuses which would not be pensioned by the main scheme.

It is important to recognise that the Inland Revenue will only allow the sacrifice of income before it is earned. For salaries this is relatively straightforward, but bonuses do cause confusion. The Inland Revenue deem that a bonus is earned at a constant rate over the course of a year even though it may arise from contract completion, and is paid once a year. Consequently the bonus must be divided by 12 to determine its monthly level and sacrificed before it is earned – which means that it is sacrificed before its size is known.

The sacrifice must be carefully and completely documented. For this reason it is recommended that professional advice is provided for staff who are likely to be interested in making bonus sacrifices.

Additional benefits

A group pension may provide benefits in addition to a member's income on retirement. These benefits include widows' and dependents' pensions, escalation of pensions, and death-in-service benefits.

For the higher-paid employee the death-in-service benefit can offer a sophisticated family protection and tax planning opportunity. The lump sum provision of four times salary is paid under a discretionary trust so that it falls outside any charge to inheritance tax. If the members' spouse has adequate provision without the lump sum then it may be more appropriate to redirect the whole or part of that sum to, say, the children, free of tax. A simple, if sizeable, example will clearly demonstrate the benefits:

Example

Assume that a scheme member dies with an estate of £1,000,000, and wishes to leave £400,000 to his children, and the remainder to his wife. On his death the pension scheme would also pay a lump sum of £400,000 to his wife. The amount passing would be:

To children

From estate	£ 400,000	
Less: inheritance tax	(£ 108,800)	
Amount to children		£ 287,200

To wife

From estate	£ 600,000	
From pension scheme	£ 400,000	
Amount to wife		£1,000,000
Total passing to family		£1,291,200

If the member reorganised his affairs so that the whole of his estate passes to his wife, and the whole of the death-in-service entitlement was paid to his children the result would be:

To children

From pension scheme	£ 400,000	

To wife

From estate	£1,000,000	
Total passing to family		£1,400,000
Inheritance tax saving		£ 108,800
(£1,400,000 − £1,291,200)		

The above example shows the potential benefits available from sensible planning, but quite often it is not practical to divide the estate as simplistically.

It could be that the member wishes to have part of the pension lump sum passing to his wife, and part to the children, but is not able to realistically make a decision about how best to make that division. If the pension scheme rules will permit, the death-in-service lump sum could be transferred to a discretionary trust which would allow for advancement of capital to wife or children as the trustees thought appropriate, so that the practical decisions could be deferred until the requirements became obvious. This is an option best accomplished with professional advice.

It should be noted that death-in-service benefits are also affected by the Finance Act 1989, so that a high earner moving jobs will almost certainly experience a significant fall in the level of protection available to his family, since the maximum lump sum under an exempt approved scheme is £259,200, though it is possible to look to unapproved schemes, as outlined later.

Personal pensions

Prior to 1 July 1988, the self-employed and those employees who were not in the company pension scheme could take out retirement

WHOLLY AND SIMPLY PORTABLE....

annuity policies. These retirement annuities were replaced on 1 July 1988 by personal pensions.

While retirement annuities are of limited interest in a book on incentivising, because only the individual, and not the company, could pay into the scheme, personal pensions will permit contributions by the company.

One of the main attractions of personal pensions to the employee is the fact that they are wholly and simply portable, and hence will not affect job mobility. This may be a good thing when seeking to recruit staff but less good when it comes to retaining them!

However, if you recognise that you are in an industry were mobility is an accepted part of career progression, eg advertising, then it may be preferable to recognise that the employee will inevitably be affected by the salary cap (currently £64,800) in a company scheme, and so allow, and assist, the greater flexibility of maintaining high inputs into the employee's own personal scheme. Continuing personal pension schemes can have a distinct advantage over an equivalent investment into many company schemes if the early termination charges can be avoided.

Company contributions, up to the allowable limit in any year, enjoy the same privileges as a company scheme contribution, namely tax relief and freedom from National Insurance. The applicable rates of contribution are as shown in Table 5.

Table 5   Personal pension contribution rates for 1990/91

Age range	Maximum rate of contributions (%)	Maximum contributions (£)
35 or less	17.50	11,340
36–45	20.00	12,960
46–50	25.00	16,200
51–55	30.00	19,440
56–60	35.00	22,680
61 or over	40.00	25,920

Unapproved pension arrangements

For many years there was an absolute limit to the amount of pension that could be funded by a scheme – namely, 2/3rds of salary. The rationale for this limit is obscure but it appears to arise from Civil Service benefits agreed during the Napoleonic Wars! This limit was abandoned in the Finance Act 1989, and replaced with two types of scheme, namely the exempt approved scheme, which currently has a pensionable salary limitation of £64,800, and enjoys tax benefits, and the unapproved scheme, which has no limit but enjoys no tax enhancements.

There are two options available in respect of unapproved arrangements – they can be funded or unfunded. Where the scheme is funded employees will suffer an immediate tax charge on contributions made on their behalf, and the fund will suffer income and capital gains tax. On withdrawal of benefits income will be fully taxed, though cash can be taken without a charge. If the scheme is unfunded then both the income and the cash will be taxed when benefits are paid.

Unapproved schemes are at the start of their life, and detailed Inland Revenue specifications are still awaited. Nevertheless, in their present guise, unapproved benefits would appear to have little to recommend them. If the scheme is funded there are double tax charges; if the scheme is unfunded it is treated no differently to ordinary pay, and is only as certain as the profitability of the company.

Portability

A considerable part of the current legislation has been directed to providing increased portability options, and better value for money transfers. Any company pension scheme should take this into account lest adverse response to poor transfer benefits erodes the positive aspects of the scheme in the eyes of the members.

In most cases this will probably mean no more than providing realistic transfer values and prompt information – the latter is a surprisingly rare commodity.

Where job mobility is a fact of life, pension portability needs to be considered in relation to scheme joiners as well as leavers. Where an employee is transferring between companies that both run money purchase arrangements there should be little problem in assigning policies across, and maintaining the contribution. This will have the positive effect of eliminating early termination charges; it could however mean that within a few years the level of administration has increased dramatically if everyone belongs to different insurance companies.

Offering professional advice on the best way to utilise transfer values will have increasing importance in the future when the best possible benefits will be required from retained benefit policies.

Contracting out

A decision about contracting out will in the future become important to the higher paid. There are two methods by which a group scheme can contract out, namely by guaranteeing to at least match the State Earnings Related Pension Scheme (known as the Group Money Purchase method), or by redirecting a portion of the National Insurance contribution (known as the Rebate Method). In both cases the scheme effectively takes into itself the State element, which has the practical effect of capping the possible pension further. It is recommended that if pension schemes are being structured to provide incentives then you will need to make maximum use of the facilities available. In order to accomplish this it would be more practical to permit the individual to contract out by means of a personal pension so that the benefits arising from it and the State are in addition to, rather than instead of, the company pension.

Quick summary

- Fundamental changes have been made to the pension regime in recent years, as a result of which employees are becoming increasingly pension aware.
- Employees earning over £64,800 may now become more reluctant to move jobs as this may have an adverse effect on pension entitlement. It is envisaged that this problem will be exacerbated over time if the salary cap limit fails to keep its value in line with salary inflation.
- Less well-paid employees are likely to be more mobile, however, due to the introduction of personal pensions and increased portability.
- Companies should consider carefully the relative attractions and disadvantages of final salary schemes and money purchase schemes.

Chapter 7

Profit-Related Pay

Background

The design of performance-related incentive schemes, otherwise known as performance-related pay (or PRP) has been considered in some depth in Chapter 1. This is, however, a very different animal to profit-related pay (confusingly, also referred to as PRP) which is a particular tax-advantageous pay scheme introduced by the Chancellor of the Exchequer in 1987. References in this chapter to PRP refer to the specific profit-related pay legislation introduced in the Finance (No 2) Act 1987 and do not apply to other forms of performance-related pay, whether calculated by reference to profits or otherwise.

Although PRP can, in certain circumstances, be a constituent of the incentive package offered to employees, it should be emphasised that PRP is not itself an incentive scheme. Many companies have been disappointed with the Government's PRP scheme on the grounds that it is unduly restrictive and cannot be utilised in their incentive planning. This is to misunderstand PRP and the context in which it was first introduced.

The philosophy behind PRP has little to do with incentive planning. Rather, the Government were primarily concerned that pay was regarded by employee and employer alike as a fixed overhead. Thus, if the economy suffered a downturn, companies would be forced to either make employees redundant or go bust. The Chancellor's view was that employees should be prepared to allow a proportion of their earnings to vary in line with company profitability. This would enable employees to enjoy the company's prosperity in the good times, but more importantly, when times were hard, wages would fall thus ensuring that the company could survive without making employees redundant.

In order to encourage more companies to set up profit-related pay

....TO ENABLE THE EMPLOYEES TO **ENJOY THE COMPANY'S PROSPERITY**
IN THE GOOD TIMES....

schemes, the Chancellor introduced a tax incentive whereby one–half of all PRP (up to certain limits - see below) would be treated as being income tax-free.

Although there was widespread interest in PRP when it was first introduced, interest amongst employers waned once the detailed provisions of the PRP scheme became known. This loss of interest was largely due to employers mistakenly thinking that they could utilise PRP as an incentive scheme, for example by paying PRP bonuses only to the extent profits exceeded targets. This is not possible – the essence of PRP is that it must vary directly in line with profits and not just some arbitrarily chosen target figure.

That having been said, some of the worst restrictions governing PRP were abolished in the Finance Act 1989, and correctly structured PRP can play an important role in incentive planning.

The basic rules

The basic provisions covering PRP are relatively straightforward. The general rule is that each participant in a PRP scheme may receive one-half of his PRP completely free of income tax up to the point where PRP is 20% of his total pay (including the PRP referrable to that period) or £4,000 per year, whichever is the lower.

It should be noted that there is no similar exemption from National Insurance contributions.

Examples

1. Fran earns £10,000 and is paid PRP of £2,000. The maximum PRP that would attract tax relief is the lower of 20% of £12,000 (ie £2,400) and £4,000.

    As the actual PRP receipt is within the PRP limits, one-half of the PRP (ie £1,000) will be completely tax free. As she is a basic rate (25%) tax payer, Fran will have saved £250 tax.
2. Colin earns £30,000 and is paid PRP of £5,000. The maximum PRP that could attract tax relief is the lower of 20% of £35,000 (ie £7,000) and £4,000.

    The amount of PRP on which he can obtain tax relief is therefore restricted to £4,000. One-half of that amount (ie £2,000) will be tax free. As Colin is a higher rate (40%) taxpayer, his actual tax saving will be £800.

Registration

1. For payments made under a PRP scheme to qualify for tax relief, the scheme must be registered before the start of the first profit year. Registration must be applied for on the standard application form PRP10 (see Appendix 3).
2. The scheme employer must sign a declaration that the scheme complies with the requirements of the PRP legislation.
3. An independent accountant must sign a report that in his opinion the scheme complies with the PRP legislation and that the books and records the scheme employer keeps or proposes to keep will enable the employer to make an annual return (including a further accountant's report) for each profit period.
4. The application form states that the scheme rules should not be sent to the PRP office unless requested. Nonetheless, it is advisable to submit the scheme rules and the PRP office have confirmed that they will comment in appropriate cases.
5. The Inland Revenue guarantee to register any PRP scheme before its proposed start date provided it meets the necessary conditions and application is made more than three months before the start date. In practice the Inland Revenue will register the scheme

within a few weeks. Application cannot be made more than six months before the start date.

Requirements of a PRP scheme

The scheme rules must be in writing and must identify both the scheme employer and the employment unit. The employment unit may be a group of companies, a single company, or even a branch or division of a company. The employment unit must be one in which business is carried on with a view to profit.

The scheme rules must clearly identify the employees to whom it relates. All employees may be included except those with a 'material interest' in the company. Broadly speaking, an employee will have a material interest if he (together with associates) owns more than 25% of the ordinary share capital.

Certain employees may be excluded if so desired: these are part-timers and new recruits. The scheme employers may choose their own definition of part-timers and new recruits, subject to the following limits:

- Part-timers – employees who are not required, under the terms of their employment, to work in the employment unit for 20 hours or more a week.
- New recruits – employees who have not been employed by a relevant employer for a period of three years.

Subject to the above exclusions, the terms of the scheme must provide that no payments are made if, at the beginning of the profit period, less than 80% of employees in the employment unit are eligible to participate.

Ascertainment of the distributable pool

The distributable pool must be determined by reference to either Method A or Method B. Under Method A the distributable pool is a fixed percentage of profits. Under Method B a notional sum is chosen and this is then increased or decreased in line with profits. The relationship can either be exact (so that a 10% increase in profits gives rise to a 10% rise in the distributable pool) or proportional (for example, so that a 10% rise in profits leads to a 5% increase in the distributable pool). The fraction limiting the effect of annual changes cannot be less than one-half and must be used for both increases and decreases and applied each year to the percentage difference. The effect of the fraction is to smooth out peaks and troughs as profits fluctuate.

The scheme may provide for profits over a certain limit to be disregarded. The ceiling must be specified in the scheme but can never be less than 160% of the previous period. For a Method B scheme with the maximum limiting fraction of one-half, it is possible to limit the annual increase in the distributable pool to 30%.

The scheme may also provide for a lower limit for profits below which no PRP will be paid. It is often sensible to have a lower limit to avoid the inconvenience of making very small payments.

The whole of the distributable pool must be paid to the eligible employees. Interim payments may be made on account but in this case a final adjustment will be necessary when the actual profits are known.

It is sensible to make interim payments on a conservative basis as excess tax relief may be recovered by the Inland Revenue from the scheme employer.

All employees must be entitled to participate on similar terms. However, it is not clear what this means and an Inland Revenue Statement of Practice would be welcome. It is clear that each employee need not receive the same amount and individual payments may be varied to reflect length of service, levels of remuneration, or similar factors. The extent to which payments may be varied is not clear and in cases of doubt attention should be drawn to this area when submitting the application form.

Ascertainment of profits

The scheme must provide for the preparation of a profit and loss account to be submitted to the Inland Revenue with the company's annual return.

Where the employment unit is a branch or a division it will be necessary to include notional charges between the unit and the rest of the business. Formal invoicing is not essential but the independent accountant must be able to give a 'true and fair' opinion.

The profit and loss account must be prepared in accordance with schedule 4 to the Companies Act 1985 even if the employment unit is not a company. However no deduction may be made for the remuneration of any person who is excluded from the scheme by virtue of having a material interest.

The basic profit figure is profit on ordinary activities after taxation but this may be adjusted to either include or exclude the following:

- Interest receivable and similar income
- Interest payable and similar charges
- Goodwill

- Tax on ordinary activities (but not penalties)
- Research and development costs
- PRP
- Employer's NIC on the PRP
- Extraordinary income and/or charges
- Extraordinary profit or loss
- Tax on extraordinary profit or loss.

The scheme must provide that accounting policies must be consistent and no changes may be made if profit or loss would be affected by more than 5%.

Cancellation

The Inland Revenue may cancel the scheme with effect from the start of the first profit period where either:

- The scheme or the application did not comply with the requirements of the legislation when it was first registered, or
- Method B is used and there is a loss in the twelve months preceding the start date as no calculation of percentage increase in profits can be made.

The registration may be cancelled from the start of a profit period if:

- Method B is used and a loss is incurred
- Emoluments (excluding PRP) fall foul of the minimum wage legislation
- An annual return is not made within the time limit (normally 10 months but 7 months for public companies)
- The scheme employer so requests
- The employer changes but an application has not been made (or accepted) to change the scheme employer
- It appears the scheme will not be administered in accordance with its terms or the legislation.

Registration may be cancelled from a specified date during a profit period if there is a ground for cancellation (for example a change in circumstances including a change of scheme employer) and the scheme employer so requests.

Quick summary

A quick summary of the main rules governing the operation of PRP is given below:

- Most employers can establish a PRP scheme.

- The scheme must be registered in advance with the Inland Revenue.
- 80% of all employees must be included, although part-timers and new recruits may be excluded.
- Any employee with a material interest must be excluded.
- PRP must vary in line with audited profits.
- Eligible employees must participate on similar terms.

As can be seen from this quick summary, the restrictions are not unduly onerous. When PRP was first introduced there were a number of unwieldy restrictions, including one that the total amount expected to be paid to employees in the first year of operation had to amount to at least 5% of payroll. Many companies dismissed PRP for this reason as it would have meant either employees taking a cut in basic pay or the employer footing an extra 5% payroll bill. Fortunately, the 5% rule has been abolished and there are now no 'de minimis' provisions whatsoever.

Chapter 8

Share Incentives Generally

Background

The increasing use of shares and share options to attract, retain, and motivate employees is without doubt one of the most important developments in incentive planning in the 1980s.

Although companies have been using shares to reward key employees for many years, these schemes have typically been limited to senior management. However, more and more companies, possibly encouraged by the success of recent privatisation issues, are now realising the benefits of widespread employee share ownership. In addition, although there is little statistical evidence, it would appear from experience that companies are now extending the use of their senior share schemes to cover a far wider range of employees.

The rules governing the taxation of employee share schemes are complex and are examined in greater detail later in this chapter and the two following chapters. However, for the purposes of background information it is probably sufficient to state that employee share schemes fall into two categories – share option schemes and share participation schemes. Within each of these categories it is possible to establish either approved schemes (which enjoy favourable tax treatment but which are subject to certain restrictions) and unapproved schemes (which are more flexible but do not enjoy the same favourable tax treatment).

Share options and share incentive schemes are an important feature of corporate life for a growing number of employees. Executive share schemes are almost universal among quoted companies, whereas wider employee share schemes tend to be most popular among the largest companies. The total number of employees who participate in share option or incentive arrangements is estimated to be in excess of two million.

Source: Monks Database

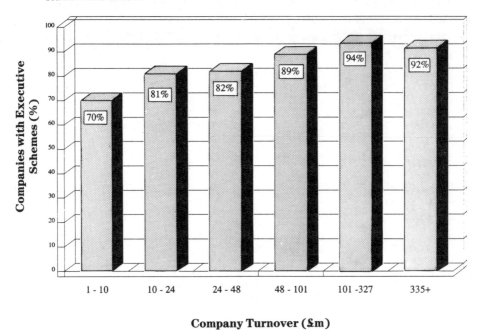

Figure 4   Incidence of executive share schemes relative to company turnover

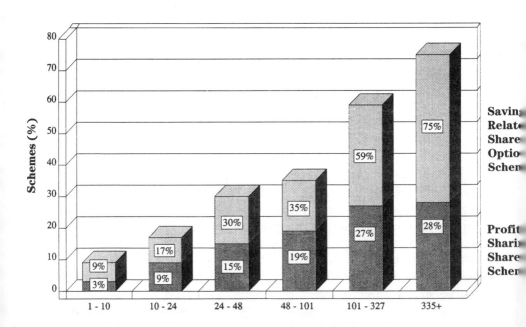

Figure 5   Incidence of wider share schemes relative to company turnover

Although the percentage of companies with all-employee share schemes seems low in comparison to the number with executive schemes, it is clear from experience that companies tend to introduce an executive scheme first and will only subsequently consider introducing an all-employee scheme.

Perhaps predictably, the available evidence suggests that all-employee share schemes are most popular with the larger companies, when measured both by number of employees and by market capitalisation (see Figures 4 and 5).

It is clear that employee share ownership is set to increase noticeably over the coming years. Employee share ownership is actively encouraged by the City and institutional investors. It also enjoys a degree of cross-party political support normally reserved only for matters of the gravest national importance. In short, there is a political consensus that employee share ownership should be encouraged. This aspect is discussed further in Chapter 10.

Incentivising with shares

Although employee share ownership is one of the least visible of all incentives, it can also be one of the most effective. This is because the potential rewards arising from participation in an employee share scheme can be quite substantial.

By participation in a share scheme, the employee becomes a part-owner (or potential owner) of the company for which he works. As a result, he can enjoy the capital rewards that flow from owning a 'piece of the action'. It is not uncommon for employees to make 'life-changing' gains from employee share schemes and they are possibly the only way in which employees can have a realistic chance of accumulating capital.

Recent surveys of new flotations in 1988 and 1989 ('Employee participation in flotations' by DJH Cohen of Paisner and Co, Solicitors) found that where share options were granted more than six months before flotation the average discount was approximately 70% of market price. In several cases the discount was over 90%. Even where the gap between the date of grant of the share option and the flotation date was between one and three months, a substantial discount could often be achieved.

It is clear therefore that employee share schemes can provide very substantial rewards to employees. Carefully structured, these rewards can be used to create powerful incentives. But incorrectly structured, they can cause major disruptions as employees use their new-found wealth to leave their employer and set up in business on

their own account, possibly in competition with the former employer.

In order to maximise the efficiency of employee share ownership schemes, the scheme should be used so as to provide both a performance incentive and a loyalty handcuff.

It is relatively easy to achieve both objectives. The grant of an employee share option can be made conditional upon certain specified targets so that the employee will only be entitled to an option if those targets are met. It is also possible to make the exercise of the options conditional upon further targets being met, so that even when the employee has been granted the option, he will not be entitled to exercise the option and hence acquire the shares at the option price until the performance target (or 'exercise condition') has been met.

Most share option schemes will provide that the option can only be exercised between certain dates (known as the 'window period'). In most cases employees are not allowed to exercise their options for the first three years following the date of grant, with the option lapsing if they leave employment. As a result, employees are effectively locked in to the company with the golden handcuff becoming more effective as the value of the shares (and hence the potential gain) rises over time.

The problem of an employee leaving immediately after exercising his option has been referred to above. One of the effects of preventing employees exercising their options for a predetermined period of, normally, three years is that income is effectively turned into capital. Where an employee is paid an annual bonus (perhaps equal to the increase in share values), that bonus has an income nature in the eyes of the recipient and is often frittered away on domestic expenditure.

The position is however very different where the employee does not receive an annual bonus but instead enjoys a capital gain at the end of the three-year period equivalent to three annual bonuses all together. The employee's lifestyle will not have adjusted for the higher standard of living as would be the case had an annual bonus been paid. The lump sum received is therefore seen by the employee as a one-off capital receipt and may be used by him to radically alter his lifestyle, for example, by leaving his current employer and setting up in competition!

This scenario can be avoided by phasing the exercise of options over a period of years. Thus, even when the employee realises a gain on the exercise of an option, he will not be tempted to leave as by so doing his remaining options would lapse.

Unapproved schemes

There is a substantial body of legislation dealing with the taxation implications of employee share ownership. The central thrust of this legislation is to ensure that any benefits from share ownership which arise as a result of the employment should be chargeable to income tax rather than capital gains tax. Although much of the impact of this legislation has been lost following the alignment of income tax and capital gains tax rates in 1988, no understanding of employee share incentives can be complete without reference to the taxation implications.

General rules

The first general rule is that where an employee acquires shares by reason of his employment at a price less than market value, he will be immediately chargeable to income tax by reference to the discount. It is irrelevant whether the employee subscribes for new shares or whether he acquires them from an outgoing shareholder. For example, an employee who is given shares in the company for which he works by an existing shareholder would be subject to income tax on the value of the shares gifted to him.

The normal presumption will be that if an employee acquires shares in the company for which he works, then he will have acquired them by reason of his employment. This will not however always be the case and there will be circumstances (for example where there is a family relationship) where the shares have been gifted for other reasons.

In addition, in certain specified circumstances a charge to income tax can arise in respect of the future growth in value of the shares. This can either happen if restrictions have been placed on the shares and are subsequently removed or varied (in which case the charge to income tax is calculated by reference to the enhanced value created by lifting the restriction) or where the shares are in a company which is a 'dependent subsidiary'. In this latter case, the entire growth in value of the shares for a period ending on the earlier of the date of disposal and the seventh anniversary of the date of acquisition will be subject to income tax. It is beyond the scope of this book to examine the detailed provisions of the dependent subsidiary legislation. Suffice it to say that the legislation is very widely drawn and will catch all subsidiary companies other than those that are wholly independent operations. Even a wholly independent subsidiary will still be deemed to be dependent (and hence subject to the growth in value charge) unless both the directors of the company and its auditors sign an annual declaration that the company is independent.

Unapproved share options

A share option is, quite simply, a right granted to a person which entitles him to acquire the underlying shares at a predetermined price and during a specified period. For example, an employee might be granted an option to subscribe for 1,000 shares at a price of £1.50 per share at any time between the third and seventh anniversaries of the date of grant.

The tax treatment of unapproved share options depends largely on whether the option arrangement is capable of exceeding seven years. If the option cannot exceed seven years (for example, because it lapses on the seventh anniversary of the date of grant) no charge to income tax arises on the date of grant. This is the case even if an option is granted to subscribe for shares at less than their current market value.

Thus there will be no immediate charge to income tax whatsoever. A charge to income tax will however arise when the option is exercised and the shares acquired. The income tax arising will be calculated by reference to the difference between market value of the shares at the exercise date and the price paid for them under the option arrangement.

When the shares are ultimately sold, a charge to capital gains tax will arise (subject to the annual exemption), calculated by reference to the difference between the sale price and market value at the date of exercise.

If, on the other hand, the option is capable of exceeding seven years the value of the option will be subject to income tax at the date of grant. A deduction for this amount will however be allowed in computing the income tax liability on the date of exercise. Thus the total amount chargeable to tax remains the same in either case but the timing of the tax liability varies.

Under an approved share option scheme (see Chapter 9), there will normally be no charge to tax until the shares are sold. At that date, a capital gain arises calculated by reference to the increase in value between the price paid under the option agreement and the ultimate disposal consideration. No liability to income tax arises whatsoever, provided the options are exercised between the third and tenth anniversaries of the date of grant and not within three years of a previous date of exercise that attracted the favourable tax treatment (see page 84).

Example

Denise is granted an option to subscribe for 1,000 shares at £2 each. The shares have a market value of £5 when the option is exercised and are eventually sold for £8.

The difference between £8 and £2 will be taxed irrespective of which option arrangement is entered into. But the type and timing of the tax charge will depend on the terms of the option.

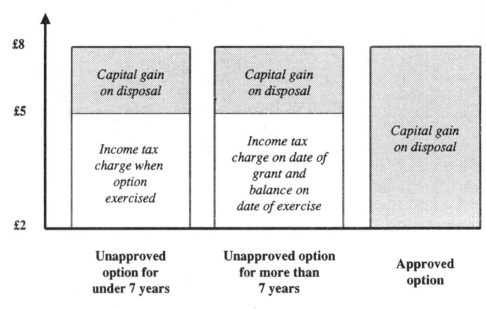

As can be seen by the illustration above, under an unapproved scheme, income tax will be chargeable on the value of the option at the exercise date less the amount paid under the option agreement, and capital gains tax will be paid on any subsequent increase in value (less indexation allowance) up to the date of disposal. The timing of the income tax charge will be brought forward if the option is capable of exceeding seven years by reference to the value of the option at the date of grant.

Under an approved scheme, no charge to tax will arise until the date of disposal, at which date there will be a charge to capital gains tax in respect of the increase in value over the period.

Approved or unapproved?

Following the alignment of the rates of income tax and capital gains tax in 1988 the question is often asked – what are the benefits of having an approved scheme? The position is certainly much more finely balanced now than when income tax rates were 60% and capital gains tax only 30%, and companies should consider carefully the relative attractions of each scheme.

A brief summary of the advantages and disadvantages of approved and unapproved schemes is set out below:

Timing	–	As has been explained above, under an approved scheme no tax liability will normally arise until disposal.
Tax	–	There is a £5,000 annual exemption from CGT (effectively doubling from April 1990 when each spouse will have a separate exemption). Also, it is possible that the rate of income tax may be increased in the future or a preferential rate of capital gains tax introduced.
Option period	–	An approved option can run for ten years without any tax liability arising. An unapproved option capable of lasting for more than seven years may give rise to a tax charge on the grant of the option.
Flexibility	–	An unapproved option can be made far more flexible than an option granted under an approved scheme. There is no need for restrictions on who can participate or the extent to which they can participate.

It should be noted that as an income tax charge arises under an unapproved scheme on the date of exercise, such a scheme will actively encourage employees to sell shares shortly after acquisition (in order to fund the tax liability). Companies anxious to encourage employee share ownership may prefer approved schemes so that no tax charge arises until disposal.

Conversely, in private companies, existing shareholders may wish to place restrictions on employee-held shares which would not be allowable under the terms of an approved scheme. In such circumstances, an unapproved scheme may be more appropriate.

Phantom share options

In some circumstances, it is either not possible or not appropriate to offer employees equity in the company for which they work. This may be due to the fact that the company is family controlled or because there may be institutional opposition to an employee share scheme (this might be the case for the subsidiary of a quoted company). In such cases, a practical solution is to establish a 'phantom' share option scheme.

In reality, a phantom share option scheme is little more than a bonus scheme dressed up to look like a share scheme. The employee is granted a phantom option to buy shares at current market value. The employee can exercise his option at any time during the window period of the scheme and is treated as having sold the shares at the market price then ruling. The company pays the employee a bonus equal to the gain he made on his phantom option.

Thus a phantom scheme is a straightforward concept and is simple to administer. Shareholder approval is not required and the company should normally obtain a tax deduction in respect of the bonus paid on the exercise of the option. It is, however, a cash scheme and will thus have a negative impact on both cash flow and profits.

The bonus is treated as income in the hands of the recipient and PAYE and NIC are due in the normal way. However, given the alignment of the rates of income tax and capital gains tax, phantom schemes may become more widespread. The major disadvantage is that the employee does not have an actual equity stake in the company and may feel that the phantom scheme is something of a second-best solution.

The need for ceremony revisited

The importance of 'ceremony' in running any incentive scheme has been discussed in general terms in Chapter 1. Ceremony is equally important in share scheme design and a number of the more practical aspects are discussed in further detail below.

Many share option schemes offer little in the way of an option certificate other than a typed sheet of paper. If the intention is to impress upon the employee the value of the benefit that has been offered to him or her, it seems pointless to detract from that impression with what will often look like a worthless piece of paper. The better approach is to prepare a formal option certificate which has been well designed and printed on rigid paper. If the option certificate is valuable (which hopefully it should be) it should look as if it is. Once again, it is the employee's *perception* of the value of the incentive that is important. The actual value is far less important.

For similar reasons thought should be given to the price which the employee should pay for the grant of the option. Under most option schemes, the grant of the option is in consideration of the payment of a nominal sum (typically £1). The payment of consideration is a legal technicality in order to ensure the existence of a binding contract. (Although no consideration is necessary where the option is granted under seal).

The payment of a nominal £1 for the grant of an option may in some cases diminish the perceived value of that option to the employee. In such cases, it may be appropriate to charge £50 or £100 for the grant of the option so that the employee realises and remembers that he has been given a valuable right.

How to get rich quick!

As has been stated above, the only way most employees will ever be able to make substantial capital profits out of their company is by participating in a share option scheme. In order to maximise the rewards that can be made (and hence maximise the incentive effect) the following ground rules should be followed:

- Grant options as early as possible
- Grant options prior to float
- For sharesave schemes, grant options at 80% of market value (see Chapter 9)
- For unquoted companies, take professional advice in negotiating the share valuation.

It has already been mentioned that the average discount where options are granted more than six months before flotation has been found by one survey (see page 73) to be 70%. This is equivalent to offering employees the opportunity to buy shares worth £1 for a price of 30 pence. It is perhaps of little surprise then that the same survey found that out of a total of 122 companies surveyed, 18 individuals made paper gains on flotation in respect of their share options of over £250,000.

Most of those options would not however have been exercisable for some considerable time and would have lapsed if the employees had left their employment. A powerful incentive not to move job indeed!

Quick summary

- The rules governing the taxation of employee share schemes are exceptionally complex and professional advice should always be taken.
- Over 80% of all publicly quoted companies have an Inland Revenue approved executive share option scheme and some 30–40% had an all-employee share scheme of one form or another.
- There is clear evidence that all-employee share ownership is more popular among larger companies.
- There is a political consensus that employee share ownership should be encouraged.

- Share schemes are possibly the only way employees can make 'life-changing' gains while retaining the security of employment.
- Share schemes can be used as both a performance incentive and a loyalty handcuff.
- It is envisaged that more and more companies will introduce unapproved schemes following the alignment of the rates of income tax and capital gains tax in 1988.

Chapter 9

Approved Employee Share Schemes

Executive share option schemes

Most companies contemplating introducing a share option scheme to incentivise or motivate key executives will automatically think of the executive share option scheme introduced by the Finance Act 1984.

The executive share option scheme is the only Inland Revenue approved scheme which can be used on a selective basis. The other approved schemes (see below) must be open to all employees (subject to certain exceptions for part-timers and new recruits) and must be operated on a 'similar terms' basis. In essence the other schemes are egalitarian in nature whereas the executive scheme is unashamedly élitist. It is also the one which allows the employees the greatest opportunity to make substantial capital profits.

The executive scheme is by far the most popular of all Inland Revenue approved schemes. This is borne out by the Inland Revenue's own statistics of the number of schemes of each sort established since inception (see Table 6).

Table 6   Inland Revenue approved share schemes

	Number of schemes submitted	Number of schemes formally approved
Profit-sharing schemes	1,200	903
Sharesave scheme	1,068	914
Executive schemes	5,778	4,449

As at 30 June 1990.

The term 'executive share option scheme' is a misnomer and is not used in the legislation. It is however the phrase used in common parlance and hence for ease of reference will also be used in this book. Executive share option schemes are open to all employees, not just executives, but in practice it is normally just the senior management who are offered options under the scheme.

The basic requirements governing executive share option schemes are extremely straightforward.

- All directors and employees are eligible to participate, with the exception of part-timers and, if the company is 'close', those who have a 'material interest'. Part-timers are defined as those who work less than 20 hours per week (25 hours for directors). A person will have a material interest if he, together with associates, controls more than 10% of the shares.
- The directors may select who is to be granted options, at their absolute discretion.
- The option must be granted at a price not manifestly less than market value. In practice, this means market value.
- No individual may hold unexercised options at any point in time with an original value in excess of four times 'relevant emoluments' or, *if higher*, £100,000.
- Relevant emoluments are, broadly speaking, all earnings paid subject to PAYE (ie excluding benefits in kind, pensions, etc) for either the current or preceding tax year.
- There are no statutory time limits for the exercise of options. However the favourable tax treatment (see Chapter 8) will only be available if the options are exercised within the seven-year window between the third and tenth anniversaries of the date of grant and not within three years of a previous date of exercise. An exception to this rule is, however, made in the case of death.
- Options may be granted at any time during the life of the scheme. Quoted companies will, however, normally restrict the period in which options can be granted to 42 days following the announcement of the company's interim or final results.

It should be noted that quoted companies will normally comply with the stricter guidelines imposed by the institutional investors. The guidelines laid down by the Investment Committees of the Association of British Insurers and the National Association of Pension Funds are set out in Appendices 4 and 5 respectively. Quoted companies will also need to comply with Stock Exchange Requirements (Appendix 6) and the Model Code for Securities Transactions by Directors of Listed Companies.

The Inland Revenue have published specimen rules for an approved executive share option scheme (Appendix 7). These rules will not, however, be suitable for all companies without some modification and professional advice should be sought where appropriate.

Profit-sharing schemes

The approved profit-sharing scheme introduced by the Finance Act 1978 is also something of a misnomer. The company can decide at its discretion how much it wishes to pay into the scheme and there need be no relation whatsoever between the amount contributed and the level of profits. Indeed, there need not be any profits at all.

From the employees' point of view the approved profit-sharing scheme is particularly favourable. Employees are entitled to receive each year under the scheme up to 10% of salary or £2,000 if higher, subject only to an overriding limit of £6,000.

The scheme is, however, an egalitarian one. All employees with five years' service (or such lower period as the directors decide) must be allowed to participate. Participation must be on 'similar terms', for example by reference to length of service, level of salary, or similar factors.

The incentive effect of a company-wide profit-sharing scheme is open to debate, although there is evidence to suggest that companies that share profits tend to outperform those that do not. It is suggested, however, that maximum benefit will be obtained from the scheme if the share ownership aspects are strengthened through good employee communication.

The way the scheme works is as follows. The company establishes a specifically constituted profit-sharing trust into which it makes a cash contribution. The payment made by the company into the trust is tax deductible.

The trustees then use the funds provided to them to either subscribe for new shares or acquire existing shares in the company. It should be noted that where the trustees use the funds to subscribe for new shares, the scheme is actually cash flow *positive*. The company makes a tax-deductible payment to the trustees but is immediately returned the money in a tax-free form (ie as subscription monies for new shares). Hence for every net £65 paid out, £100 is returned.

The shares held by the trustees are appropriated to individual employees on whatever similar terms basis the scheme rules allow. Although the shares are held by the trustees, the employees may still enjoy the benefits of share ownership. Dividends will flow directly through to the employees and they may instruct the trustees how to vote their shares.

The shares *must* be retained by the trustees for a period of two years. They *may* be released to the employee after the expiry of two years but they can only be released on an income tax free basis if they are retained by the trustees for a further three years (that is, five years in total). There is a 25% taper relief from income tax if the shares are released in year five. Special rules apply where an employee disposes of his shares in the five-year period because of retirement, redundancy, or disability.

An illustration of the workings of a profit-sharing scheme is set out in Figure 6.

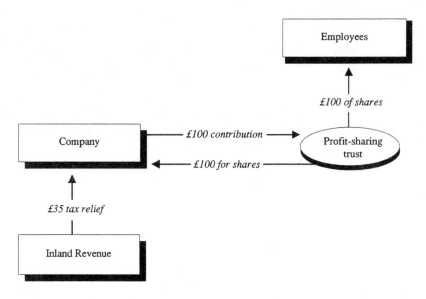

Figure 6   Approved profit-sharing scheme

Buy one, get one free

Another, but conceptually very different, version of the profit-sharing scheme is the matching offer scheme. This scheme is identical to the traditional profit-sharing scheme but the allocation of shares to employees is calculated by reference to the number of shares each employee is prepared to supply or purchase out of his own resources. The appropriation of shares on this basis is accepted by the Inland Revenue as falling within the definition of 'similar terms'.

Conceptually, however, the two schemes are very different. Whereas the traditional scheme is in essence a reward scheme – effectively employees are given shares in a tax-free form – a matching offer is more akin to an investment scheme. The company is effectively encouraging its employees to buy its shares by offering them one (or more) free share for each share purchased out of their own resources.

This scheme, which can be an extremely efficient means of encouraging employee share ownership, is often known in common parlance as 'Buy One, Get One Free' (or BOGOF). Some companies have now introduced a further level of sophistication to a BOGOF scheme by arranging for the shares purchased by the employee out of his own resources to be held in a personal equity plan, thus ensuring that they grow in value in a tax-free environment.

Sharesave – you just can't lose

The facility to introduce savings-related share option schemes (colloquially known as 'Sharesave') was introduced by the Conservative Government in 1980. The attraction of the scheme was significantly boosted in the Finance Act 1989 when the maximum savings contract was increased by 50% (from £100 to £150 per month) and the discount at which options could be granted was doubled from 10% to 20%. As a result, Sharesave schemes are enjoying a major revival as more and more companies are seeing their benefits.

A Sharesave scheme has, as its name suggests, two constituent elements – a savings scheme and an employee share scheme. Under the savings element, employees are invited to enter into a Save As You Earn ('SAYE') contract. Each employee can decide how much he wishes to save, subject to a monthly minimum of £10 and a maximum of £150. Payments are made directly, by way of payroll deduction, to the selected savings institution. Until recently SAYE could only be operated by building societies or the Department of National Savings. However, the Finance Act 1990 extended this facility to banks and it is envisaged that the major clearing banks will soon become a significant force in promoting Sharesave.

Under the terms of the SAYE contract, the employee agrees to save for a fixed period of five years and will then be entitled to a tax-free bonus equal to 15 months' contributions. This is an effective tax-free rate of interest of 8.86% which for a basic rate taxpayer is equivalent to a return of 11.81%. Employees may, if they so decide, leave their savings in the Building Society or Bank for a further two years following the end of the five-year savings contract. If they do so, they will then receive an additional bonus equal to a further 15 months' contributions.

Although the rate of interest on a SAYE contract is in itself quite attractive (an 11.81% rate of return fixed for five years), the real attraction of Sharesave lies in the opportunities offered under the Share Option Scheme element. At the time the employee enters into his SAYE contract, he will also be given an option to use his accumulated savings to acquire shares at the end of the five (or seven) year period. The price at which he can buy the shares can be set at a generous 20% discount to their value at the date the option was granted. Thus the employee's savings are guaranteed, but at the same time he has the opportunity to make a possible substantial capital profit.

The Sharesave scheme must be open to all full-time employees who have completed five years' service with the company. Other employees may be invited to participate at the company's discretion.

The savings contract permits up to six monthly contributions to be missed and, provided they are made up later, each missed contribution simply delays the bonus date by one month.

There are numerous attractions of Sharesave to employees, including:

- It provides an opportunity to share in the success of the company.
- Shares can be made available at a preferential price.

- There is a guaranteed tax-free bonus on maturity of the savings contract.
- Savings contributions are deducted direct from salary.
- There is no obligation to buy the shares when the savings contract matures.
- Any gains arising from the sale of shares are usually subject to capital gains tax (where the annual exemption is often sufficient to ensure no liability to tax) rather than income tax.

From the employer's point of view the attraction of Sharesave is that it allows the opportunity of rewarding employee loyalty (options lapse if the employee leaves) at no cost to the company, other than a small degree of equity dilution. In addition, the launch of the scheme to employees (which is normally handled free of charge by the savings carrier – see below) may of itself increase employee awareness of the company for which they work.

Further, the company can encourage its employees to enter into a regular savings contract, so that at the very least the employees will have invested 'rainy day' money in a Building Society or bank account. Hopefully, however, the company's share price will grow substantially above the option price (which can be as low as 80% of current market value) thus allowing the employees to enjoy substantial rewards for their loyalty.

The workings of a Sharesave scheme are illustrated diagrammatically in Figure 7.

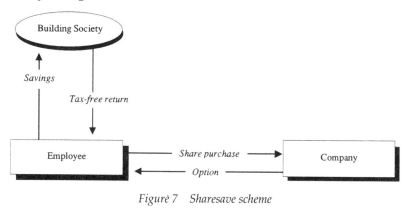

Figure 7   Sharesave scheme

Example

Sandy is granted an option to buy shares in the company she works for at a price of 80p, which represents a 20% discount to current market value of £1. Sandy decides to take out a five-year contract and save just £20 each month.

If the shares increase in value at just 10% per annum, the share price will grow from £1 at the start of the contract to £1.61 five years later. Given that Sandy can buy the shares at 80p, she has already more than doubled her money.

The £20 saved by Sandy each month amounts to £1,200 at the end of the five-year period. In addition she will receive a tax-free bonus (equal to fifteen months' contributions) of £300. Hence she will have a total amount of £1,500 with which she will be able to buy 1,875 shares at the option price of 80p.

If Sandy sells the shares immediately at the market price of £1.61 she will receive £3,019, a gain of £1,819 on her £1,200 investment.

Bearing in mind the fact that Sandy did not invest her £1,200 at the outset but built up her saving over a period of five years, this figure of £1,819 represents an *annual* tax-free compound rate of return on her savings of 37.6% (equivalent to 50.1% for a basic rate taxpayer).

However, in a dull market, it may be unduly optimistic to expect shares to increase at 10% per annum. In fact, even if the share price had not moved at all Sandy would have enjoyed an annual compound rate of return in excess of 17.8% tax free (equivalent to 23.7% for a basic rate taxpayer). This is because of the combined effect of the bonus on the savings contract (equivalent to an annual rate of return of 8.86%) and the 20% share price discount offered under the scheme.

Easing the admin burden – at no extra cost

The major Building Societies have in the past devoted substantial resources to winning and retaining Sharesave business. From a commercial viewpoint it is easy to see why the Building Societies are anxious to promote Sharesave. A Sharesave scheme will typically introduce a large number of new regular savers to the Building Society who are saving under a long-term (five- or seven year) plan and who do not receive interest (in the form of the terminal bonus) until the expiry of five (or seven) years. It is thus an excellent source of new business for the Building Societies.

For this reason Building Societies have set up specialist units devoted to Sharesave, which typically offer the following services free of charge:

- Glossy booklets customised to companies' requirements
- Employee videos explaining the benefits of Sharesave
- Employee presentations

- Posters and in-house publications
- Administrative support for payroll and personnel arrangements
- Computer print-outs for share register and annual return
- General guidance.

Companies that take full advantage of the service offered by the Building Societies can find that the very act of introducing a Sharesave scheme is sufficient to heighten employee loyalty and identification with the organisation for which they work.

From 1 September 1990, banks will also be allowed to offer SAYE contracts and it is certain that competition between the banks and the building societies will hot up. This is likely to result in an increased level of service being offered in order to win new sharesave business. Companies contemplating the introduction of Sharesave would be well advised to shop around for the best deal in terms of the level of administrative support offered.

Quick summary

- 'Executive' schemes are by far the most widespread of all Inland Revenue approved schemes. This is primarily because the scheme is discretionary and does not have to include all employees on similar terms.
- All companies must comply with the detailed requirements set out in the legislation. In addition, quoted companies will usually follow the additional restrictions set out in guidelines issued by the various investor protection committees.
- An approved profit-sharing scheme is most attractive to employees as they can receive shares free of any income tax charge. From the company's point of view, the scheme can be cash flow positive although there will always be a negative impact on earnings per share.
- Employee commitment can be encouraged by establishing a matching offer scheme under which the appropriation of free shares is calculated by reference to the number of shares each employee is prepared to acquire out of his own resources.
- Savings-related share option schemes received a double boost in the Finance Act 1989 with the savings limit being increased to £150 per month and the maximum share price discount being doubled to 20%. As a result Sharesave schemes are enjoying a major revival.

Chapter 10

ESOPs

Background

Employee share ownership plans (or ESOPs as they are more commonly known) are one of the most exciting and innovative developments in share scheme planning for many years. ESOPs were originally devised in the United States and following enabling legislation there in 1974, they have grown to the extent that it is estimated that more than 10 million workers now participate in ESOPs.

In the United Kingdom, interest in ESOPs has grown in recent years and even before the Finance Act 1989 gave ESOPs an official seal of approval, it had been estimated that over 10,000 employees belonged to UK ESOPs.

Possibly the most remarkable aspect of ESOPs is the widespread support they engender. To date, a number of ESOPs have been set up with the backing of the Transport and General Workers' Union (TGWU) and funded by Unity Trust (the Trade Union bank). ESOPs have also been supported by the Adam Smith Institute and politicians from the whole spectrum of political opinion.

The level of support for ESOPs is best demonstrated by reading the Parliamentary Debates when ESOPs were first introduced in the 1989 Finance Bill. It goes without saying that the Conservative Party are in favour of ESOPs – after all, they introduced the enabling legislation. What is more interesting is the reaction of the Opposition parties. Hansard (6 June 1989) records Mr Nicholas Brown (Labour) as saying:

'The Labour Party is solidly in favour of employee share ownership plans. We specifically referred to them in the report of the Policy Review Group on the Productive and Competitive Economy and we referred to them with enthusiasm. The structure could lead to genuine worker control and positive and constructive participation in management decision-making. I strongly support that, and it is also supported by Unity Trust bank which has been financing ESOP schemes since 1985.'

Similarly, Mr Beith (SLD) welcomed the introduction of ESOPs with the following words:

'I welcome the provisions which will help to ease the way to the creation of more ESOP schemes. In the United States, 10 million workers participate in some 10,000 such schemes. The fact that there are fewer than 20 such schemes established in Britain suggests that we can go a long way to develop this mechanism by which workers can have a stake in the finance of their company and involvement in its ownership and control.... Aided, perhaps unwillingly in some ways, by the privatisation process which is now assuming a serious and significant role, at least in industries such as transport, it [ie an ESOP] could be a major agency for increasing the ability of employees to share in the profitability and capital appreciation of the companies they work for and for increasing their involvement in the ultimate decisions about the fate of those companies. I welcome those things and I am glad to find them in the Bill.'

As has been mentioned above, ESOPs have been around for some time now, but their development was hampered by tax uncertainties. The relief offered by the Finance Act 1989 went some way to assist the development of ESOPs but the conditions placed on the scheme were so onerous that only one company chose to follow the qualifying ESOP route. Nonetheless, the publicity surrounding the introduction of the qualifying ESOP has done much to encourage employers to establish ESOP arrangements. It is perhaps ironic that most employers will be advised to select the previous non-qualifying ESOP in preference to the qualifying version introduced in the Finance Act 1989.

In a further attempt to stimulate interest in qualifying ESOPs, the Finance Act 1990 introduced a generous form of rollover relief for vendors wishing to sell shares into an ESOP. Although this new relief is very much welcomed, it does create something of a conflict between vendors anxious to sell their shares to a qualifying ESOP in order to obtain rollover relief, and companies wishing to avoid the statutory restrictions of the qualifying ESOP.

Some public companies have discovered that conventional employee share schemes do not create long-term employee share participation. ESOPs can ensure that a significant employee stake is created and protected. In the case of private companies, employee minority share ownership has never been very attractive as there is rarely a convenient and attractive exit route. An ESOP can provide an internal share market and give employee share ownership a real boost.

How does an ESOP work?

ESOPs must be designed to meet the specific requirements of the company and its employees. No two companies are the same. However, there are usually a number of common ingredients to such plans. An ESOP consists of two basic elements – acquiring the equity stake and distributing the equity to employees.

The mechanics are as follows:

1. The company establishes a discretionary trust.
2. The trust borrows either from the company itself or, more usually, externally from a financial institution such as a bank.
3. The trust uses these funds to acquire an equity stake in the company and holds these shares for the benefit of the employees. These shares may be newly issued, thereby generating new finance for the company, or shares could be acquired from existing shareholders.
4. The shares are distributed to employees over a period of years via an employee share scheme. The employee share scheme can be either 'approved' by the Inland Revenue or 'unapproved', as the case may be.
5. As the shares are transferred to staff the trust can repay the loan. The interest on the loan can be paid off and the loan itself can be repaid in a number of ways.

For example, the proceeds of the transfer of shares to staff and the dividends arising on the shares for the time being held in the trust can be used to service the interest and the loan repayments.

Alternatively, or in addition, the company can make contributions to the trust to cover the interest and loan repayment. There was case law to support a claim for a corporation tax deduction for such contributions but until now there was no statutory right to a deduction.

The six stages of a conventional ESOP arrangement, as shown in Figure 8, are:

(1) The ESOP borrows from the bank
(2) The ESOP subscribes for new shares in the company
(3) Over time, the company makes tax-deductible contributions into an employee share scheme

(4) The employee share scheme utilises the funds in buying shares from the ESOP
(5) The ESOP repays its bank loan out of the sale proceeds
(6) The shares held by the employee share scheme are distributed to employees.

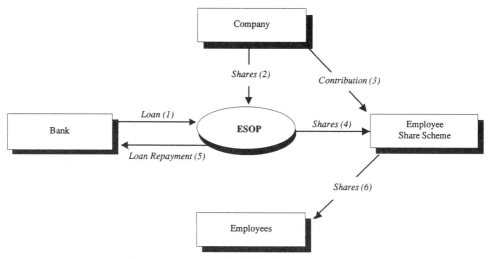

Figure 8   A conventional ESOP arrangement

Qualifying ESOPs

Under the provisions of the Finance Act 1989 a corporation tax deduction is guaranteed provided certain conditions are met. The conditions are examined in more detail below but the main areas are:

1. The company and the trustees must be UK resident.
2. The trustees must use the contributions paid to them for a qualifying purpose. 'Qualifying purpose' is any of the following:
   (a) the acquisition of shares in the company
   (b) the repayment of sums borrowed
   (c) the payment of interest on sums borrowed
   (d) the meeting of expenses.
3. The trust must use the contributions for a qualifying purpose within nine months from the end of the accounting period (or such longer period as the Inland Revenue may allow).
4. A claim for tax relief must be made within two years of the end of the accounting period.
5. There must be at least three trustees, of whom:
   (a) one trustee must be either a trust corporation or a solicitor or other professional

    (b) most of the trustees must not be and must never have been directors of the relevant company

    (c) most of the trustees must be employees who do not have a material interest and who have been selected by either a majority of the employees or their elected representatives.

6. The beneficiaries *must* include all full-time employees (at least 20 hours' service per week) who have five continuous years' service. Other employees may be included, on a discretionary basis if desired, provided they have at least one year's service. Employees with a material interest (5%) must however be excluded.

7. Any tax deduction on contributions to the trust will be clawed back from the trust if the trustees make non-qualifying transfers or if the shares are retained in the trust for more than seven years.

Qualifying or non-qualifying ?

Until the Finance Act 1989, ESOPs had no official status and therefore no tax privileges. The main problem this caused was the uncertainty as to whether corporate payments to ESOPs were tax-deductible. Under the provisions in the Finance Act 1989, all payments to a qualifying ESOT (employee share ownership trust) will be tax-deductible provided various conditions (summarised above) are satisfied. Payments or share transfers by ESOTs to employees will be subject to income tax in the employee's hands. This means that, in practice, ESOTs will almost always be operated in tandem with approved profit-sharing schemes. The ESOT will buy the shares in the first place and will subsequently sell them to the profit-sharing trust. That sale will create potential liabilities to both capital gains tax and stamp duty.

    ESOTs were given a further boost in the Finance Act 1990. Shareholders may now sell shares to a qualifying ESOT and defer their ensuing capital gains tax liability by reinvesting the proceeds in *any* replacement taxable asset.

    In order to be eligible for ESOP rollover relief, the ESOP trust must have a 10 per cent stake in the company immediately after, or within 12 months of the sale. In addition, the vendor must acquire the replacement asset within a period of six months from the date of sale, or of the 10 per cent condition being satisfied, if that is later. The deferred gains will become taxable when the replacement assets are disposed of.

    Companies wishing to set up ESOPs will have to decide whether the certainty of a tax deduction is sufficient compensation for the loss of flexibility which compliance with the qualifying conditions will entail. Although some companies have in the past obtained deductions for payments into ESOPs it is possible that once an approved route is available the Inland Revenue will take a harder line with those who continue to use the non-approved method.

It is not however possible to set up a qualifying ESOT in conjunction with an executive share option scheme or a Sharesave scheme. Also it is often beneficial to ensure that the ESOP trust is resident in a low tax area. This is not possible with a qualifying ESOT as it is a requirement of the ESOT legislation that the trustees must be UK resident. As a result, many companies will continue to prefer non-qualifying ESOPs despite the tax uncertainties.

ESOPs as a poison pill

One of the more common uses of ESOPs in the United States has been as a poison pill to stave off the possibility of takeover. In essence, the

... TO ENSURE THE SHARES DO NOT FALL INTO **UNFRIENDLY HANDS**....

ESOP builds up a significant stake in the company's equity in order to ensure that shares do not fall into unfriendly hands.

The use of ESOPs in bid defence is highly controversial in the US and it would certainly not be perceived well in the City (and may also be void under UK company law) if an ESOP was established specifically for the purposes of making a company bid-proof.

That having been said, there are strong commercial, economic, and social reasons for allowing employees a say in their company's future through the medium of an ESOP trust. Consider, for example, the take-over bid by Nestlé for Rowntree, where a strong regional workforce was effectively disenfranchised and the ultimate fate of Rowntree lay in the hands of City-based institutions.

Had Rowntree had an established ESOP, the views of the employees (presumably more concerned about long-term job security than share price) would have been a more important factor in the bid and the result might well have been different.

This is not to single out Rowntree (who are, of course, a company renowned for employee welfare) but merely to point out that ESOPs can have a legitimate role in bid-defence, especially where there are extraneous factors involved (such as regional issues).

The use of ESOPs in bid-defence should, however, be carefully monitored and advice taken regarding Takeover Panel, Stock Exchange, and legal implications.

Captive shares

One of the major attractions of ESOPs is that shares can be captured at a low price (for example, in a management buy-out or flotation situation) for subsequent disposal to employees over a period of years. Thus, all employees may be able to benefit from the initial low price, even if it was either inappropriate or impossible for them to do so at the time.

For example, in a management buy-out, it is not normally possible for the workforce generally to be party to the negotiations and hence it would be impractical for them to be included in the buy-out agreement. Increasingly, however, management teams are establishing ESOPs so that the trustees can be a party to the purchase agreement, thereby acquiring shares at the buy-out price for subsequent distribution to employees.

The advantages of an ESOP acquiring the shares (rather than the employees directly) is twofold. First, as explained above, the use of an ESOP can greatly simplify the mechanics of employee involvement. Second, the ESOP can acquire shares for the entire class of employees – including future employees. Obviously, this would not be possible if the existing employees acquired shares directly at the time of the buy-out.

A new tool in corporate finance

ESOPs can also have an important role in corporate finance. As a result of amendments to the Companies Act financial assistance provisions introduced specifically to assist the spread of ESOPs, ESOP trusts will be able to borrow funds from external sources (guaranteed by the company) and use the funds to subscribe for new shares in the company.

This is of particular interest for a number of reasons. First, the company is raising finance by issuing shares to a new 'institutional' shareholder – that is, employees generally. Second, the loan is effectively off-balance-sheet as the person taking out the loan is the ESOP and not the company.

Third, and possibly most important, the repayment of the loan will be funded out of payments into the ESOP, which payments should be tax-deductible. Hence, the company is effectively obtaining a tax deduction for repayment of the loan capital as well as the interest element.

A number of lending institutions are now fully aware of the attractions of ESOPs and many are now actively beginning to exploit the market. As a result, is it likely that the emergence of ESOP lending will be a major new trend over the coming months and years.

ESOPs as a marketmaker

ESOPs are not the exclusive province of quoted companies. In fact, the major ESOPs to date (Roadchef, Yorkshire Rider, MFI) all concerned private companies. ESOPs can play an important role in creating an internal share market where otherwise there would be no ready market in the company's shares.

Consider, for example, a family company that wishes to provide employees with a share in the equity. Employees may be reluctant to purchase shares where there is no readily ascertainable exit route. Conversely, the family may be happy for employees to hold shares but would be unwilling to allow an employee to retain shares in the event of his leaving.

Carefully structured, an ESOP can prove to be an ideal solution. The ESOP trust can buy and sell shares on its own account, thus creating an internal market in the company's own shares. The ESOP can also act as a point of contact by collating details of employees wishing to buy and sell shares and arranging transfers on a matched bargain basis.

An alternative to flotation

The advantages of ESOPs outlined above can together combine to make ESOPs an interesting alternative to flotation for many private companies. The recent trickle of public companies (such as Virgin Group plc, Charles Church plc, Really Useful Group plc, etc) leaving the stock market has made many potential quoted companies aware that flotation is not necessarily the best solution for all companies.

Many larger private companies will however be pressurised to float for a number of reasons, including:

- Raising new capital
- Employee participation
- Realisation of funds by major shareholders.

All the above pressures to float could be alleviated (to a greater or lesser extent) by establishing an ESOP. The ESOP could be initially funded by a substantial loan with the proceeds being used to subscribe for new shares (thus raising new capital) and to acquire shares from existing shareholders (thus realising cash for the vendors). In addition, the ESOP will by its very nature increase employee share participation.

That having been said, there are numerous other factors involved in the flotation question which could not necessarily be solved with an ESOP. In particular companies planning a rapid expansion through acquisitions funded by way of share issue may consider that a stock market listing is the only viable alternative.

Quick summary

- Interest in ESOPs has grown as companies have sought to emulate the US ESOP experience. The Finance Act 1989 gave ESOPs an official seal of approval.
- Under the provisions of the Finance Act 1989, all payments to a qualifying ESOP will be tax-deductible provided various conditions are met.
- A shareholder selling shares to a qualifying ESOT will be eligible for rollover relief provided certain conditions are met.
- A tax deduction may still be available under general principles for contributions to a non-qualifying ESOP.
- Companies wishing to set up ESOPs will have to chose whether the certainty of a tax deduction is sufficient compensation for the loss of flexibility which compliance with the qualifying conditions will entail.

- ESOPs can be used for a wide variety of purposes, including the creation of an internal share market and as an alternative to flotation.

Appendix 1

The Taxed Award Scheme

2 November 1984   *Inland Revenue*

Incentive Awards and Prizes for Employees: Taxed Award Schemes

(Crown copyright. Reproduced by kind permission of the Inland Revenue)

The Board of Inland Revenue has recently approved new voluntary arrangements for collecting tax on non-cash incentive prizes awarded to employees. These arrangements will be open to the providers of non-cash awards and provide an alternative and simpler method of collecting tax on such awards than the existing procedure of collecting the tax directly from the recipient.

Under the new scheme providers of such awards to their own employees or to the employees of third parties will be able, if they wish, to arrange with the Inland Revenue to cover the recipients' basic rate tax liability on the grossed-up value of the award by entering into a legally binding contract which provides for the grossing-up arrangement and the payment of the related tax together with simplified reporting arrangements. The arrangements do not cover any higher-rate liability which may arise from the receipt of the award (which tax will continue to be collected directly from the taxpayer) nor do they cover the award of cash prizes or cash vouchers assessable under PAYE in accordance with the instructions in paragraph 28 of the *Employers' Guide to PAYE*. Recipients of any award should continue to include details of the award on their own tax returns.

These arrangements are voluntary and are intended only for award schemes which are designed for employees. A special Valuation Unit has been established to deal with the valuation of incentive awards and to set up Taxed Award Schemes.

A note designed to give producers further details of the Taxed Award Scheme arrangements may be obtained from Inland Revenue, Incentive Valuation Unit, New Wing, Somerset House, London WC2 1LB. Telephone: 071 - 438 7253 or 071 - 438 7329.

Notes

1. Incentive prizes awarded to employees for reaching sales or performance targets, etc, are assessable to tax under Schedule E. Where the prize is other than cash or a cash voucher the measure of the liability to tax will usually be the cost of providing the award. The exact figure may however depend on the details of the scheme and whether the recipient is 'higher-' or 'lower-paid' for the purposes of the benefits-in-kind provisions contained in FA 1976, Part III, Ch.2, (now ICTA 1988, Part V, Ch.2).
2. At present the liability on non-cash awards is collected directly from the recipient on the basis of a notification from the provider. Cash awards and cash vouchers are paid under deduction of tax through the PAYE system.
3. The new arrangements which are made by the Board of Inland Revenue under their statutory powers for the care and management of the tax system are designed to provide an alternative and simpler method of collecting tax on non-cash awards made to employees. The new arrangements are entirely voluntary and are restricted to providers making such awards through schemes designed for employees.
4. Under the new arrangements providers will be able, if they so wish, to cover the recipients' basic rate tax liability on the grossed-up value of the award. Any higher rate tax liability will be collected from the recipient in the usual manner. The scheme also includes a simplified reporting procedure for providers and enables the recipient to receive notification of the value of the award and the tax paid on his behalf. (*Author's note:* The Taxed Award Scheme was extended to cover higher rate liability with effect from 18 January 1990.)

Appendix 2

Suggestion Schemes

8 August 1986   *Inland Revenue Concession (A57)*

Awards to employees under suggestion schemes

(Crown copyright. Reproduced by kind permission of the Inland Revenue)

Income tax will not be charged under Schedule E in respect of an award scheme made by an employer to an employee under a staff suggestion scheme where the following conditions are satisfied:

(a) There is a formally constituted scheme under which suggestions are made and which is open to all employees on equal terms.

(b) The suggestion for which the award is made is outside the scope of the employee's normal duties. The test is whether, taking account of his experience, the employee could not reasonably have been expected to have put forward such a suggestion as part of the duties of his post. Where meetings of employees are held for the purposes of putting forward suggestions, they should be regarded as part of their duties and any consequential awards would not be within the terms of this concession.

(c) Awards other than encouragement awards (see (g) below) are only made following a decision to implement the suggestion and are made directly to the employees concerned.

(d) The decision to make an award other than an encouragement award is based on the degree of improvement in efficiency and/or effectiveness likely to be achieved measured by reference to:
   (i) the prospective financial benefits and the period over which they would accrue, and
   (ii) the importance of the subject matter, having regard to the nature of the employer's business.

(e) The amount of an award does not exceed:
   (i) 50% of the expected net financial benefit during the first year of implementation, or

(ii) 10% of the expected net financial benefit over a period of up to 5 years, subject to an overriding maximum of £5,000. Where an award exceeds £5,000 the excess is not covered by this concession.

(f) Where a suggestion is put forward by more than one employee the award made under (e) above is divided between them on a reasonable basis.

(g) Any encouragement award is of £25 or less. An encouragement award is one which is made in respect of a suggestion which, though it will not be implemented, has some intrinsic merit and/or reflects meritorious effort on the part of the employee in making the suggestion.

This concession does not apply to any liability to income tax or capital gains tax on income or gains arising from the exploitation or disposal of rights in an invention devised by the employee, eg patent rights, know-how, etc.

Registration Form For Profit-Related Pay

**Inland Revenue
Profit-Related Pay Scheme**

Application for Registration

Please read the enclosed Notes on Completion before you start to fill in this form.
The numbers on the left hand side of this form refer to these notes.

You may also find it helpful to read the Inland Revenue booklet PRP2 "Tax Relief for Profit-Related Pay: Notes for Guidance" before you begin.

Please ask the Profit-Related Pay Office (PRPO) if you need any further assistance or information about completing this form. If you find there is not enough room in any part of the form please attach a separate sheet.

To have your scheme registered you need to complete parts 1-3, 4 or 5 and, if appropriate, part 6 of this form. When you have signed the declaration in Part 7 and your independent accountant has completed the report in Part 9, please send the form to the PRPO at the address shown on page 4.

Please also give the statistical information requested in Part 8.

Part 1   General information   *(please use capital letters)*

See Note

1 **Employer's Accounts Office PAYE reference no - *as shown on the Payslip Booklet***

| | | **P** | | | | | | | |

2 **Scheme employer's name**

Address

Postcode _____

Your ref *if required*   **Your Tel no**

3 **Type of business** *use the appropriate code number*

4 **Employment unit specified in PRP scheme.** *Please clearly identify the unit - if necessary by defining the activities/operations.*

5 **Communications to agent** *tick this box if required*

6 **Agent's name**

Address

Postcode _____

Agent's reference   **Agent's Tel no**

Part 2   Scheme employee details

See Note
7   Please enter the estimated number of employees to whom the scheme will relate at the start of the profit period

Full time [   ]   Part time [   ]

Part 3   Timing of PRP payments
Note 8

8   What is the basis on which payments are made under the scheme? *Tick one box*

Annually only   Interim with annual adjustment

[   ]   [   ]
            Monthly or more frequently   [   ]   *Less frequently than monthly*

Part 4   Profit period and distributable pool details
Note 9

See Note

10-11   Start date of first profit period [| |]   End date of first profit period [| |]

12-13   Duration of scheme [   ] year(s)   If no limit specified [   ]
                                                          in scheme tick here

14   If the scheme covers only a **part** of the undertaking but the
       PRP pool is to be calculated by reference to the profit or   [   ]
       loss of the **whole** undertaking, please tick the box

15-16   **Please fill in only one of the boxes below**

Method A	Method B
17-18 Is the fixed percentage to be applied to profits known? *Tick one box* [Yes] [No]	Is the amount of the notional pool known? *Tick one box* [Yes] [No]
If **Yes**, enter that percentage [%]	If **Yes** enter that amount [£]
If **No** please send a full description of the method by which the percentage is to be fixed.	If **No** please send a full description of the method by which the amount is to be determined.
19 Does the scheme provide for a lower limit of profits below which there will be no PRP pool? *Tick one box* [Yes] [No]	Does the scheme provide for a lower limit of profits below which there will be no PRP pool? *Tick one box* [Yes] [No]
20 Does the scheme provide for an upper percentage limit beyond which any profits will be disregarded? *Tick one box* [Yes] [No]	Does the scheme provide for an upper percentage limit beyond which any profits will be disregarded? *Tick one box* [Yes] [No]
21	Does the scheme provide for any fraction to be applied in calculating the PRP pool? *Tick one box* [Yes] [No] If "Yes" enter that fraction [ ]

Part 5   Replacement schemes

Note 22

See Note

Please state for each registered PRP scheme to be replaced by the proposed scheme:

PRP reference

23 Details of the change including the circumstances which give rise to it, as a ground for cancellation.

Date of the change

24 Whether the registration has already been cancelled
Tick one box

Yes ☐   No ☐

If **No**, whether

a request for its cancellation has been made ☐

written notice that it may require cancellation has been given ☐

If **neither**, please state the present position

25 Confirm that at least one half of the employees to whom the scheme relates at the start date are employees to whom a registered PRP scheme related at the time of the change, leading to the cancellation of its registration?

Yes ☐

26 Start date of first profit period

End date of first profit period

Number of profit periods *Tick one box*

1 ☐   2 ☐

27 Please state the percentage of profits specified in the scheme rules to be used to calculate the size of the distributable pool

☐ %

Part 6   Group scheme employer only *(list all companies included in the   scheme with their Accounts Office PAYE reference number - if appropriate)*

Name	Address	Employer's Accounts Office PAYE ref no

3

Part 7 Scheme employer's declaration
Note 28

See Note

No employment to which the scheme relates is an excluded employment as defined in Section 174 of the Income and Corporation Taxes Act 1988.

The scheme, the rules of which are set out in writing, complies with the requirements of Sch 8 to the Income and Corporation Taxes Act 1988 as amended and to the best of my knowledge and belief the particulars given on this form are correct and complete.

The emoluments paid to any employee in the scheme and to whom minimum wage legislation applies will satisfy that legislation without taking account of profit-related pay.

Signature _____ Date _____

29 | Capacity in which signed _____
(Secretary, Treasurer, Partner, Proprietor etc)

Part 8   Statistical information

See Note

30 Please enter an estimate of the annual pay (excluding PRP) of the employees covered by the scheme   £

If you have chosen method A please state what the size of the distributable pool will be if profits remain the same as in the latest year for which profits are known.   £

If you currently operate for the majority of employees a profit-based cash bonus scheme, the payments of which do not qualify for tax relief, state the percentage of the pay bill that the payments represent.   %

Part 9 Independent accountant's report
Note 31

In relation to the scheme for (name of employment unit)_____

to which this application relates I am/we are (an) independent accountant(s) as defined in Section 184 of the Income and Corporation Taxes Act 1988.

I/We have examined the scheme, the rules of which are set out in writing, and have considered the administrative arrangements proposed by the applicant. In my/our opinion the scheme complies with the requirements of Sch 8 to the Income and Corporation Taxes Act 1988 as amended and the books and records maintained and proposed to be maintained by the applicant are adequate for the purpose of enabling the documents required by Section 180(1) of the Income and Corporation Taxes Act 1988 to be produced.

Signature _____ Qualification _____

Name/address _____

_____

_____ Postcode _____ Date _____

When completed send this form to: **Profit - Related Pay Office**
Inland Revenue
St Mungo's Road
Cumbernauld
Glasgow G67 1YZ

For official use only

Date processed

Initials

Do **not** send the scheme rules with this application form. They may be called for at a later date together with supporting records and information.

4

Printed in the UK for HMSO Dd 8154810 C500 10 89 5200 12521

(Crown copyright. Reproduced by kind permission of the Inland Revenue)

Appendix 4

Employee Share Schemes – ABI Guidelines

Association of British Insurers Investment Committee: share option and profit-sharing incentive schemes: revised guidelines to requirements of insurance offices as investors

(Reproduced by kind permission of the Association of British Insurers)

Summary of revision

The Association of British Insurers has reviewed the operation of the guidelines [ie, the Guidelines to Requirements of Insurance Offices as Investors] in the light of developing practice and the recent successes in persuading companies to adopt performance criteria as a condition for the exercise of options. Profit-sharing arrangements are already linked to performance and the Association has sought to devise performance criteria which will require sustained improvement in the underlying performance of a company as a condition for the exercise of all options other than options linked to a savings contract.

The guidelines now make provision for the inclusion in executive share option schemes adopted in the future of a minimum performance requirement that options should only be exercisable if during the option period there has been a real growth in the company's earnings per share. Provision is also made for the grant of options by a company over more than 5% of its ordinary share capital and in excess of four times the annual emoluments of the participant, provided that such additional options shall normally be exercisable not earlier than five years from the date of grant and then only if the growth in earnings per share of the company over any five year-period following the date of grant has been such as places the company in the top quartile by reference to the growth in earnings per share of the FTSE 100 companies. Arrangements which involve a participant holding options over more than four times emoluments at any one time should require performance of a specified and demanding amount in place of the minimum real growth requirement.

In all cases such arrangements are subject to the overall limit of 10% of a company's ordinary share capital for all employee share schemes in any ten-year period with a maximum participation in the same period by any one individual of eight times annual emoluments.

It has been felt sensible to incorporate a provision that in future options should be granted by an independent committee of the board and preferably by a committee of non-executive directors, who will not themselves participate in the options. It will be expected that this committee will satisfy itself with regard to options exercised that the various performance requirements have been met on a consistent basis, ie the requirements are not achieved by the inclusion of extraordinary items or creative accounting.

In circumstances where the annual remuneration of senior employees already includes a substantial element of performance-related pay, consideration should be given to the inclusion of an overall cap limiting the maximum individual participation in order to avoid an excessive amount of options being granted to any one individual. Details of options granted in any one year should in future be included as a specific item in the report and accounts with a statement of the number of employees participating in a company's scheme.

It is believed that such schemes should provide a clear community of interest between employees and the shareholders and that this is best achieved by the grant of options only over the share capital of the parent equity thus ensuring that any benefit received by the employee is available equally to the shareholders.

Arrangements which involve the grant of options over the share capital of a subsidiary company will normally be opposed therefore unless in the case of an overseas subsidiary the employee would be precluded by local legislation from participating or, in the case of a UK subsidiary, at least 25% of its ordinary share capital is quoted on a recognised exchange and held outside the group.

The guidelines, which replace those issued by the BIA Investment Protection Committee in April 1985, are intended to ensure that where share option arrangements are proposed there will be a real incentive to produce sustained growth in a company's performance, and a community of interest between participants and shareholders. The framework of schemes which are consistent with the spirit of the guidelines should ensure that the share capital earmarked for such schemes will be available to employees as widely as possible and be adequate to meet all reasonable needs of a company in this context. Consideration will of course be given to a situation where the circumstances are not covered by the guidelines.

Revised guidelines

The guidelines to employee share option schemes have been revised to reflect evolving practice and to incorporate for the first time performance requirements as a condition of the exercise of any option (other than an option granted pursuant to an SAYE scheme which is available to all employees). The requirements set out below outline the restrictions which insurance offices regard as essential under such schemes if excessive appropriation of the equity entitlement of ordinary shareholders is to be avoided.

Insurance offices have a duty on behalf of policy holders and others on whose behalf they invest to permit only those schemes which make available such an appropriation of the profits and share capital as is felt to be equitable having regard to the finance provided by the proprietors of the company in the past and their reasonable expectations of growth in the future. The Committee believes that the method of providing incentive arrangements in any company is a matter for its management and that the directors will take account of all the interests concerned in formulating the particular schemes proposed which, in all cases involving the issue of equity capital, should be submitted to shareholders for approval.

However, as judgement of the incentive effects of particular arrangements involving the equity capital of a company is essentially a matter for its shareholders, observance of all requirements set out below will not necessarily ensure support for schemes which shareholders may feel are inappropriate on other grounds. The guidelines are intended to indicate the basic provisions necessary to give general effect to the principles outlined above in the hope that any scheme proposed which is consistent with the spirit as well as the letter of the requirements will ensure a genuine community of interest between shareholders and scheme beneficiaries. The main objectives of the guidelines are to ensure that over a period of ten years no more than 10% of the shareholders' equity is utilised for schemes of all kinds and that options which are not linked to SAYE savings contracts may be exercised only if there are accompanying and genuine long-term benefits to the company. Furthermore, in order to conserve the benefits under such schemes for future participants, no more than 3% of the equity should normally be appropriated for all forms of scheme in any three-year period. In order that shareholders may review the effectiveness of option arrangements, schemes should have a life of not more than ten years.

Accordingly, unless there are very exceptional circumstances, insurance offices will be recommended to oppose proposals for the adoption of any scheme which does not satisfy each of the following requirements.

Profit-sharing schemes

(1) The aggregate of the amount of the equity share capital of the proposing company that may be issued in any calendar year by way of subscription under profit-sharing schemes may not exceed 1% of such share capital in issue on the day preceding the appropriation of profits for the purpose of the scheme as set out under Requirement (3).

(2) The aggregate of the amounts that may be appropriated out of profits in any calendar year for all profit-sharing arrangements involving the acquisition by subscription or purchase of the company's shares may not exceed 5% of that proportion of the profits of the relevant trading period before tax and excluding any exceptional items which, in the opinion of the directors, is attributable to the operation of participating employees. Whenever the amount so appropriated would subscribe at the price calculated in accordance with Requirement (4) more than the amount of share capital permitted under Requirement (1), the balance of such appropriation may be applied in the purchase of shares in the market.

(3) The appropriation of profits for profit-sharing schemes shall be made once only by the directors after announcement of the final results for the trading period in respect of which the appropriation is made and paid over to the trustees of the scheme as soon as practicable.

(4) The price at which shares are subscribed under Requirement (1) shall be the middle market price of the shares of the same class on the dealing day prior to the appropriation of profits under Requirement (3).

(5) On any occasion when part of any appropriation under Requirement (3) is applied in the purchase of shares in the market, the price at which shares are made available to participants under the scheme shall be the average per share of the cost of the shares subscribed under Requirement (4) and the cost including expenses of the shares purchased.

(6) Any monies received by the trustees for the acquisition of shares shall not be retained but shall be applied as far as practicable forthwith in the subscription or purchase of shares for immediate appropriation to the individuals eligible under the scheme.

(7) Any monies received by the trustees by way of dividends on the shares held in trust shall not be retained but shall be distributed immediately to the individual to whom the relevant shares have been appropriated.

(8) On any occasion when the voting rights attached to the shares held in trust fall to be exercised, the trustees shall obtain the instructions of the individuals to whom the relevant shares have been appropriated and exercise the voting rights accordingly.

Option Schemes

(9) Except as provided in (10) and (11) below, the amount of ordinary share capital issued or issuable pursuant to all options schemes, other than schemes linked to an SAYE contract, shall be limited to 5% of the ordinary share capital at the time a participation is granted and such options should normally be exercisable only if there has been a real growth in the earnings per share of the company over a three-year period following the date of grant. In appropriate circumstances up to a further 5% may be set aside for such schemes provided that any options over shares in excess of 5% of the issued ordinary capital shall be exercisable not earlier than five years from the date of grant and

normally then only if the company's growth in earnings per share over a period of at least five years has been such as would place it in the top quartile of the FTSE 100 companies by reference to growth in earnings per share over the same period. The aggregate share capital issued or issuable by the company under all share option or profit-sharing schemes within the preceding ten years must not exceed 10% of the ordinary share capital of the company at any time when a participation is granted.

(10) In the case of a company having a market capitalisation of £5m or less, up to 10% of the equity capital when aggregated in accordance with (9) above may be issuable under the scheme provided that the market value of such capital does not exceed £500,000 at the time of the adoption of the scheme.

(11) The market value at the relevant time of the share capital to be appropriated, by allotment or by options granted, to any one participant when aggregated with the market value at the time of appropriation of any share capital appropriated in the preceding ten years to that participant under the proposed or any other share option schemes (other than an SAYE linked option) must not exceed four times the participant's total annual emoluments from the companies within the scheme and there should be a condition that such options will normally be exercisable only if, over any three-year period from the date of grant, the company has achieved as a minimum a real growth in earnings per share.

In appropriate cases options having a market value of up to a further four times a participant's annual emoluments may be granted if such additional options are exercisable not earlier than the fifth anniversary from the date of grant and normally then only if the company's growth in earnings per share over a period of at least five years following the date of grant has been such as would place it in the top quartile of the FTSE 100 companies by reference to growth in earnings per share over the same period.

In the case of schemes approved by the Inland Revenue under the Finance Act 1984 [ie, executive share option], and which do not provide option linking arrangements, options granted up to 1 October 1979 under other schemes may, for the purpose of the individual participation limit, be disregarded and options granted under other schemes after 1 October 1979 but before the adoption of the proposed scheme may be taken into account at one half of the market value of the relevant shares at the date of the grant.

(12) The price at which shares are issued to participants, or at which participants are given an option to subscribe, must not be less than the middle market price of the shares in question (or similar formula) at the time when the participation is granted which must be within a period of

42 days following the date of publication of the results of the grantor company.

(13) No option may be granted for more than ten years or exercised within three years from the date of the grant in the case of those options subject to a real growth in earnings per share requirement, or within five years from the date of grant for those options subject to top quartile growth in earnings per share requirements. In the event of a take-over of the grantor company or the death or cessation of employment of the participant, options may be exercised or lapse within one year or within three and one-half years from the date of grant, whichever is the later, unless arrangements have been made for the option to be converted, in the event of a take-over, into options of the offeror company. No option may be granted within the two years preceding the normal retirement date of the participant either under his contract of employment or otherwise and not later than ten years from the date of the adoption of the scheme.

(14) Participation under the proposed scheme must be restricted to directors or employees who are required to devote substantially the whole of their working time to the business of the grantor company or its subsidiaries, and options, which must be non-assignable, may normally be granted only over the share capital of the parent company. As a general rule any arrangement involving the grant of options over a subsidiary company will be opposed unless in the case of an overseas subsidiary where necessitated by local legislation or in appropriate circumstances where at least 25% of the share capital of the subsidiary is quoted on a recognised stock exchange and held outside the group.

Savings-related schemes

(15) The proposed scheme must provide that in the period of ten years commencing at the date of its adoption the total amount of share capital issued or issuable under any savings-related scheme when aggregated with the total amount of share capital issued or issuable under any profit-sharing or option scheme in the preceding ten years, whether or not approved under the Finance Acts [now Income and Corporation Taxes Act 1988], shall not exceed 10% of the equity share capital of the company at the time when capital is issued or issuable under the proposed scheme. 'Issuable' share capital includes any share capital in respect of which options have been granted or rights may be exercised.

(16) Participation under the proposed scheme may be granted only within a period of ten years from the date of its adoption.

(17) The price at which participants are given an option to subscribe must not be less than the middle market price of the shares of the class under option at the time when the option is granted unless the scheme has received Inland Revenue approval under statutory provisions relating

to contractual savings schemes, in which event the option price must be not less than 90% [now 80%]of such middle market price.

(18) No part of the equity share capital may be issued or issuable to participants for subscription out of the proceeds of a contractual savings scheme except as provided under (15) above.

(19) The maximum amount that may be contracted for savings by individual participants under the scheme shall not exceed £150 per calendar month.

General

(20a) To conserve benefits for future participants all schemes must normally provide that not more than 3% of the equity capital may be appropriated for options or subscribed out of profits under all relevant schemes in any year and the two preceding years.

(20b) In the year of introduction of any scheme or schemes otherwise complying with the above requirements and linked to an SAYE contract and available to all employees generally, the restriction under (20a) need not be observed provided that the percentage of equity capital appropriated for any options or subscribed out of profits under all relevant schemes in any year and the four preceding years does not exceed 5% and provided that options which are not linked to SAYE arrangements shall remain subject to the limit of 3% as under (20a).

(21) All options (other than linked to an SAYE contract) should preferably be granted by a committee of non-executive directors of the company or at least by an independent committee of directors who will not themselves participate in the options. This committee will be expected to satisfy itself that prior to the exercise of options, relevant performance criteria have been fully satisfied on a consistent basis, ie they have not been achieved by 'creative accounting' or by the inclusion of inappropriate or extraordinary items, and they are accountable to shareholders for such. In appropriate circumstances it would be expected that such a committee will impose an overall cap on the maximum participation under option arrangements by any one individual.

13 July 1987

Addendum to share option and profit-sharing scheme guidelines

Following representations by a significant number of the larger companies in the UK, all of whom expressed complete support for the guideline limit of 5% of capital for executive share option schemes, the ABI Investment Committee has agreed to consider a relaxation of guideline (11) in certain circumstances. This would have the effect of allowing the grant following exercise of existing options of replacement options in excess of the guideline limit of four times earnings without requiring satisfaction of the top quartile eps [earnings per share] growth provision as a condition for their exercise. Consideration would be given to the amendment of existing schemes to incorporate this revised approach.

This relaxation would be subject to the following minimum conditions:

(1) The scheme must be administered by and the grant of options supervised by a remuneration committee consisting wholly or mainly of non-executive directors.

(2) In the case of an existing scheme the total of options granted within four years from the date of the amendment shall not exceed 2.5% of the issued ordinary share capital of the company with any balance within the overall 5% limit remaining available for the unexpired term of the scheme, if any.

   In the case of a new scheme it would be envisaged that the 2.5% could be utilised in the first four years of the scheme with the remaining 2.5% being available for the remaining six years.

(3) The remuneration committee must, prior to granting replacement options, be satisfied that there has been a significant improvement in the performance of the company over the two to three years preceding the regrant.

(4) The chairman of a company making any such amendment should emphasise that the 5% limit for the executive share option scheme over a 10-year period is entirely appropriate and adequate for such purposes. He should also address the importance placed by offices as investors on underlying performance by a positive statement that replacement options will be granted having regard to the performance of the company.

In any cases where it is desirable, the yearly basis on which the above limit is calculated may, for the purposes of the scheme, be that of the financial reporting year.

6 May 1988

The following letter from the Secretary of the Association of British Insurers Investment Committee accompanies the above addendum.

I enclose a copy of an addendum to the guidelines which has been designed to assist those companies whose usage of options is modest in that no more than 5% of the company's capital will be used in any 10-year period for such purposes and where the options are granted by a remuneration committee, a majority of which comprises non-executive directors.

One of the main objects of the revised guidelines issued last year, was to incorporate in the framework of the guidelines provision for 'super options or replacement options' subject to performance requirements related to the top quartile of the FTSE 100 companies. You will note that the modification in the addendum provides that any performancing requirements shall be imposed by and monitored by the remuneration committee as a condition of regrant. In those cases where companies wish to reserve more than 5% in any 10-year period for share option arrangements or where they do not demonstrate by adopting the alternative arrangements in their entirety that 5% will be adequate for the full 10-year period, then the top quartile earnings per share test remains as set out in the revised guidelines.

It is hoped sincerely that these amendments will be seen as providing the desired flexibility for those companies whose modest usage of share capital for incentivisation is provided for under arrangements which, by limiting participation through options to 5% of the company's capital in any 10-year period, enable the framework of general schemes such as SAYE or profit-sharing schemes to be made available to employees generally.

11 May 1988

APPENDIX 5

Employee Share Schemes – NAPF Guidelines

The National Association of Pension Funds Limited, Investment Committee: Statement on Share Schemes

(Reproduced by kind permission of the National Association of Pension Funds Ltd)

The approach of institutional shareholders to the issuing of shares to employees through share schemes has evolved through many years. The NAPF last pronounced on the subject in November 1984. Its statement at that time was in the form of guidelines to potential issuers setting out practices which were not acceptable in general to the membership of the NAPF.

Since 1984 there has been a significant increase in the number of schemes which the NAPF has been asked to consider because, in the view of the management, either a particular definition required clarification, or special circumstances justified overriding a particular guideline.

To cope with this increase, and hopefully to move forward the debate in this general area, the NAPF has reappraised its attitude to share schemes. Central to this article is the following statement of the NAPF's view of the desirable objective of share schemes:

> The NAPF supports the movement to greater ownership by employees in the company within which they work. It regards this movement as long term in nature, and will support legislation designed to encourage long-term ownership of the resulting shares within a fair tolerance of the inevitable dilution effect of its members' interest in those companies.

Against this objective, the use of share schemes solely to achieve tax-efficient short-term remuneration is a disappointing development. The NAPF strongly supports profit-related pay, bonuses and other similar remuneration incentives, and regards these as more appropriate short-term measures than the use of share schemes with quick exercise rights. Such schemes are deficient in the extent to which sudden fluctuations in share price, well beyond the ability of employees to influence, either enhance or devalue the remuneration aspect. However, this is a risk those using share schemes in this way must be prepared to accept.

With this clear objective as a base from which to proceed, the NAPF states below the principles against which it views such schemes.

(1) The NAPF wishes to encourage the use of share schemes amongst employees to achieve long-term employee ownership of companies. Its members recognise that this will result in a dilution of pension funds' equity stakes, but consider that this may be acceptable where it leads to a greater coincidence of interest between shareholders, management, and employees.

(2) The NAPF wishes to encourage Boards to permit the widest possible participation in such schemes to the greater overall benefit for the company and the individuals concerned.

(3) Together with the objective of achieving long-term employee ownership, the NAPF wishes to encourage the incorporation of an incentive element relating to performance. Share price is, of course, at times a very imprecise measure of the success of companies, but exercise should only be possible at or above the price of the share when the option was granted. Furthermore, when managements wish to introduce share incentive arrangements which would not qualify under the Finance Act 1984 (ie Inland Revenue approved selective share option schemes) for taxation of the individual benefits at capital gains tax rates, it would expect a highly explicit form of performance criterion to be met.

(4) The NAPF will in general support schemes which result in a 10-year period in a maximum of 10% of ordinary share capital being made available for all share schemes in aggregate, and which in any one year during a 10-year period would result in a maximum of 5% ordinary share capital being made available.

(5) The NAPF supports those companies which give a committee of non-executive directors responsibility for monitoring and approving the operations of such schemes, and urges all those making use of such schemes to follow this practice.

(6) The NAPF has been associated with a number of initiatives to increase the flow of information available to shareholders through annual reports and accounts. Accordingly, the NAPF urges that annual reports and accounts should provide shareholders with the details of option schemes including information on the number of shares issued and issuable, prices at which options have been granted, and the number of participants.

(7) The NAPF urges that in recommending share schemes to their shareholders, Boards comment on the extent to which a particular scheme will operate within these general principles and state that in their opinion:

'the scheme is consistent with the general principles for such schemes recommended by the NAPF.'

(8) Where Boards wish to propose a scheme which departs from these general principles, Boards should explain to shareholders the particular reasons why in their opinion shareholders should nevertheless support the scheme.

With the publication of these general principles, the NAPF hopes to encourage share schemes and give relative certainty that schemes conforming to these general principles will be supported.

The NAPF is aware that the Association of British Insurers (ABI) have detailed guidelines on this general subject, about which they consulted the NAPF constructively. That the NAPF has chosen to comment in a different manner should lead no one to see its approach as undermining the stance taken by the ABI.

The NAPF will continue to respond to its members' requests for assistance in respect of share schemes. It will not, as a normal practice, comment as an Association on individual share schemes other than in response to members' requests. The NAPF expects that its members, in carrying out their duties as trustees and shareholders, will examine all share schemes, judging them in the light of these general principles.

This letter supersedes all previous statements made by the NAPF on this subject.

Appendix 6

Employee Share Schemes – Stock Exchange Requirements

(Reproduced by kind permission of The International Stock Exchange, London, from Section 1, paragraph 9 of its publication 'Admission of securities to listing – the Yellow Book.')

9. EMPLOYEE SHARE SCHEMES

9.1 The following provisions apply, with appropriate modifications, to all schemes involving the issue of shares or other securities (including options) by domestic companies to, or for the benefit of, employees. They apply also to schemes of all subsidiaries of listed domestic companies, even if the subsidiary is incorporated and operating abroad.

The Department must be consulted on the application of these provisions to schemes intended to apply to employees of associates.

9.2 (a) The scheme, which must be approved by shareholders in general meeting, must contain provisions relating to:-

　(i) the persons to whom or for the benefit of whom securities may be issued under the scheme ('participants');

　(ii) the total amount of the securities subject to the scheme which must be stated together with the percentage of the issued share capital that it represents at that time;

　(iii) a fixed maximum entitlement for any one participant (if the scheme is subject to any statutory maximum entitlement, that maximum from time to time will be permitted);

　(iv) the amount, if any, payable on application or acceptance and the basis for determining the subscription or option price, the period in or after which payments or calls, or loans to provide the same, may be paid or called; and

　(v) the voting, dividend, transfer and other rights, including those arising on a liquidation of the company, attaching to the securities and to any options (if appropriate). These rights must be drawn to the attention of participants on their joining the scheme.

(b) The scheme or corresponding document, if not circulated to the shareholders, must be available for inspection for at least 14 days in the City of London or such other places as the Committee may agree.

(c) The terms of the resolution must approve a specific scheme and refer either to the scheme itself (if circulated to the shareholders) or to a summary of its principal terms included in the circular which must contain all the provisions set out in sub-paragraph (a). Where directors of the company are trustees of the scheme or have an interest direct or indirect in the trustees, the circular must disclose that interest.

(d) (i) Unless the securities subject to the scheme are identical with other listed securities they must be separately designated.

(ii) A scheme may provide for adjustment of the subscription or option price or the number or amount of securities subject to options already granted and to the scheme, in the event of a capitalisation issue, a rights issue, sub-division, consolidation of shares or reduction of capital. Such adjustments should give a participant the same proportion of the equity capital as that to which he was previously entitled.

(iii) The issue of securities as consideration for an acquisition will not be regarded as a circumstance requiring adjustment.

(iv) Adjustments, other than those made on a capitalisation issue, must be confirmed to the directors in writing by the company's auditors to be in their opinion fair and reasonable.

(v) The scheme must provide, or the circular must state, that the provisions relating to the matters contained in (a) and (d) (ii) above cannot be altered to the advantage of participants without the prior approval of shareholders in general meeting.

Appendix 7

Employee Share Option Scheme – Inland Revenue Specimen Rules

(Crown copyright. Reproduced by kind permission of the Controller of Her Majesty's Stationery Office)

(Where indicated, reference should also be made to the numbered notes at the end of this Appendix.)

Rules of the [...............][1]
Employee Share Option Scheme

1. DEFINITIONS

In these Rules the following words and expressions shall have the following meanings:

'Announcement Date'	the date on which the annual or half-yearly results of the Company are announced.
'Appropriate Period'	the meaning given in paragraph 15(2) of Schedule 9.
'Approval Date'	the date on which the Scheme is approved by the Board of Inland Revenue under Schedule 9.
'Associated Company'	has the same meaning as in Section 416 of the Income and Corporation Taxes Act 1988.
'Auditors'	the auditors for the time being of the Company (acting as experts and not as arbitrators).
'Board'	the Board of Directors of the Company or, except in Rule 10.4, a duly constituted committee thereof.
'Company'	[......................][1]

'Control'	has the same meaning as in Section 840 of the Income and Corporation Taxes Act 1988.
'Dealing Day'	[a day on which the Stock Exchange is open for the transaction of business.][2]
'Date of Grant'	the date on which an Option is, was, or is to be granted under the Scheme.
'Eligible Employee'	any director or employee of any Participating Company who is required to devote to his duties not less than 25 hours (or, in the case of an employee who is not a director of any Participating Company, 20 hours) per week (excluding meal breaks) and is not precluded by paragraph 8 of Schedule 9 from participating in the Scheme.
ICTA 1988	The Income and Corporation Taxes Act 1988.
'Market Value'	[on any day the average of the middle market quotations of a Share as derived from the Daily Official List of The Stock Exchange for the 3 immediately preceding Dealing Days. (Provided that if the Dealing Days do not fall within the period specified in Rule 2, only such days as do fall within that period will be taken into account in arriving at the Market Value).][3] [On any day the market value of a Share determined in accordance with the provisions of Part VIII of the Capital Gains Tax Act 1979 and agreed for the purposes of the Scheme with the Inland Revenue Shares Valuation Division on or before that day.][4]
'Option'	a right to subscribe for Shares granted (or to be granted) in accordance with the Rules of this Scheme.
'Option Holder'	an individual to whom an Option has been granted or his personal representatives.
'Participating Company'	the Company and any other company of which the Company has Control and which is for the time being nominated by the Board to be a Participating Company.

'Relevant Emoluments'	the meaning which the terms bears in sub-paragraph (2) of paragraph 28 of Schedule 9 by virtue of sub-paragraph (4) of that paragraph.
'Schedule 9'	Schedule 9 to the Income and Corporation Taxes Act 1988.
'Scheme'	the employee share option scheme constituted and governed by these Rules as from time to time amended.
'Share'	an [ordinary]5 share in the capital of the Company which satisfies the conditions specified in paragraphs 10–14 inclusive of Schedule 9.
'Subscription Price'	the price at which each Share subject to an Option may be acquired on the exercise of that Option being, subject to Rule 8, the higher of: (i) the nominal value of a Share, and (ii) the Market Value of a Share on the day the invitation to apply for that Option was issued pursuant to Rule 2.
'Subsisting Option'	an Option which has neither lapsed nor been exercised.
'Year of Assessment'	a year beginning on any 6 April and ending on the following 5 April.

Where the context so admits the singular shall include the plural and vice versa and the masculine shall include the feminine.

Any reference in the Scheme to any enactment includes a reference to that enactment as from time to time modified, extended or re-enacted.

2. INVITATION TO APPLY FOR OPTIONS

At any time or times within a period of four weeks after an Announcement Date or the Approval Date, and in any case not earlier than the Approval Date nor later than the tenth anniversary thereof, the Board may in its absolute discretion select any number of individuals who may at the intended Date of Grant be Eligible Employees and invite them to apply for the grant of Options to acquire Shares in the Company. Each invitation shall specify:

    i. the date (being neither earlier than 7 nor later than 14 days after the issue of the invitation) by which an application must be made,

    ii. the maximum number of Shares over which that individual may on that occasion apply for an Option, being determined at the absolute discretion of the Board save that it shall not be so large that the grant of an Option over that number of Shares would cause the limit specified in Rule 5.2 to be exceeded, and

    iii. the Subscription Price at which Shares may be acquired on the exercise of any Option granted in response to the application.

Each invitation shall be accompanied by an application in such form, not inconsistent with these Rules, as the Board may determine.

3. APPLICATIONS FOR OPTIONS

Not later than the date specified in the invitation each Eligible Employee to whom an invitation has been issued in accordance with Rule 2 above may apply to the Board, using the application form supplied, for an Option over a number of Shares not exceeding the number specified in the invitation.

    [Each application shall be accompanied by a payment of £1 in consideration for the Option to be granted.][6]

4. GRANT OF OPTIONS

4.1 Not later than the twenty-first day following the issue of invitations the Board may grant to each applicant who is still an Eligible Employee an Option over the number of Shares specified in his application.

4.2 As soon as possible after Options have been granted the Board shall issue a certificate of option in respect of each Option in such form, not inconsistent with these Rules, as the Board may determine.

4.3 No Option may be transferred, assigned or charged and any purported transfer, assignment or charge shall cause the Option to lapse forthwith. Each option certificate shall carry a statement to this effect.

5. LIMITATIONS ON GRANTS

[5.1 No Option shall be granted pursuant to Rule 4 above if such grant would result in the aggregate of
    i. the number of Shares over which Subsisting Options have been granted under this Scheme and
    ii. the number of Shares which have been issued on the exercise of Options granted under this Scheme and
    iii. the number of Shares over which subsisting options have been granted under any other share option scheme during the period of 10 years ending on the relevant Date of Grant and
    iv. the number of Shares which have been issued pursuant to any other employee share scheme (including a share option scheme) during the period of 10 years ending on the relevant Date of Grant exceeding $(x\%)$ of the number of shares then in issue.][7]

5.2 No Option shall be granted to an Eligible Employee if immediately following such grant he would hold Subsisting Options over Shares with an aggregate Subscription Price exceeding the greater of
    i. £100,000 or
    ii. four times the amount of the Eligible Employee's Relevant Emoluments for the current or preceding Year of Assessment (whichever of

those years gives the greater amount) or, if there were no Relevant Emoluments for the preceding Year of Assessment, four times the amount of the Relevant Emoluments for the period of twelve months beginning with the first day during the current Year of Assessment in respect of which there are Relevant Emoluments.

For the purposes of this Rule 5.2 Options shall include all Options granted under this Scheme and all options granted under any other scheme, not being a savings-related share option scheme, approved under Schedule 9 and established by the Company or any Associated Company thereof.

6. EXERCISE OF OPTIONS

6.1 Subject to Rule 9 below any Option which has not lapsed may be exercised in whole or in part at any time following the earliest of the following events:
   i. the third anniversary of the Date of Grant
   ii. the death of the Option Holder
   iii. the Option Holder ceasing to be a director or employee of any Participating Company by reason of injury, disability, redundancy or retirement [or for such other reasons as are specified in the Rules].
6.2 An Option shall lapse on the earliest of the following events:
   i. the tenth anniversary of the date of the grant
   ii. the first anniversary of the Option Holder's death
   iii. six months following the Option Holder ceasing to be a director or employee of any Participating Company, other than by reason of his death
   iv. unless a release has been effected under Rule 7.4, six months after the Option has become exercisable in accordance with Rule 7
   v. the Option Holder being adjudicated bankrupt.

7. TAKEOVERS AND LIQUIDATIONS

7.1 If any person obtains Control of the Company as a result of making
   i. a general offer to acquire the whole of the issued share capital of the Company which is made on a condition such that if it is satisfied the person making the offer will have Control of the Company or
   ii. a general offer to acquire all the shares in the Company which are of the same class as the Shares,
   then any Subsisting Option may subject to Rule 7.4 below be exercised within six months of the time when the person making the offer has obtained Control of the Company and any condition subject to which the offer is made has been satisfied.
7.2 If under [Section 425 of the Companies Act 1985 or Article 418 of the Companies (Northern Ireland) Order 1986][8] the Court sanctions a compromise or arrangement proposed for the purposes of or in connection with a scheme for the reconstruction of the Company or its

amalgamation with any other company or companies, any Subsisting Option may subject to Rule 7.4 below be exercised within six months of the Court sanctioning the compromise or arrangement.

7.3 If any person becomes bound or entitled to acquire shares in the Company under [Section 428 to 430 of the said Act of 1985 or Articles 421 to 423 of the said Order of 1986][8] any Subsisting Option may subject to Rule 7.4 below be exercised at any time when that person remains so bound or entitled.

7.4 If as a result of the events specified in Rules 7.1 or 7.2 a company has obtained Control of the Company, or if a company has become bound or entitled as mentioned in Rule 7.3, the Option Holder may, by agreement with that other company (the 'Acquiring Company'), within the Appropriate Period, release each Subsisting Option (the 'Old Option') for an option (the 'New Option') which satisfies the conditions that it:

    i. is over shares in the Acquiring Company or some other company falling within paragraph (b) or paragraph (c) of paragraph 10, Schedule 9, which satisfy the conditions specified in paragraphs 10 to 14 inclusive of Schedule 9.

    ii. is a right to acquire such number of such Shares as has on acquisition of the New Option an aggregate Market Value equal to the aggregate Market Value of the shares subject to the Old Option on its release.

    iii. has a subscription price per Share such that the aggregate price payable on the complete exercise equals the aggregate price which would have been payable on complete exercise of the Old Option; and

    iv. is otherwise identical in terms to the Old Option.

The New Option shall, for all other purposes of this Scheme, be treated as having been acquired at the same time as the Old Option.

Where any New Options are granted pursuant to this clause 7.4, Rules 4.3, 6, 7, 8, 9, 10.1, and 10.3 to 10.6 shall, in relation to the New Options, be construed as if references to the Company and to the Shares were references to the Acquiring Company or, as the case may be, to the other company to whose shares the New Options relate, and to the shares in that other company, but references to Participating Company shall continue to be construed as if references to the Company were references to [...........................][1].

7.5 If the Company passes a resolution for voluntary winding up, any Subsisting Option may be exercised within six months of the passing of the resolution.

7.6 For the purposes of this Rule 7 other than Rule 7.4 a person shall be deemed to have obtained Control of a Company if he and others acting in concert with him have together obtained Control of it.

7.7 The exercise of an Option pursuant to the preceding provisions of this Rule 7 shall be subject to the provisions of Rule 9 below.

7.8 Where in accordance with Rule 7.4 Subsisting Options are released and New Options granted the New Options shall not be exercisable in accordance with Rules 7.1, 7.2, and 7.3 above by virtue of the event by reason of which the New Options were granted.

8. VARIATION OF SHARE CAPITAL

In the event of any capitalisation or rights issue or any consolidation, subdivision or reduction of capital by the Company, the number of Shares subject to any Option and the Subscription Price for each of those Shares shall be adjusted in such manner as the Auditors confirm to be fair and reasonable provided that:

  i. the aggregate amount payable on the exercise of an Option in full is not increased
  ii. the Subscription Price for a Share is not reduced below its nominal value
  iii. no adjustment shall be made without the prior approval of the Board of Inland Revenue and
  iv. following the adjustment the Shares continue to satisfy the conditions specified in paragraphs 10 to 14 inclusive of Schedule 9.

9. MANNER OF EXERCISE OF OPTIONS

9.1 No Option may be exercised by an individual at any time when he is precluded by paragraph 8 of Schedule 9 from participating in the Scheme.

9.2 No Option may be exercised at any time when the shares which may be thereby acquired are not Shares as defined in Rule 1.1.

9.3 An Option shall be exercised by the Option Holder giving notice to the Company in writing of the number of Shares in respect of which he wishes to exercise the Option accompanied by the appropriate payment and the relevant option certificate and shall be effective on the date of its receipt by the Company.

9.4 Shares shall be allotted and issued pursuant to a notice of exercise within 30 days of the date of exercise and a definitive share certificate issued to the Option Holder in respect thereof. Save for any rights determined by reference to a date preceding the date of allotment, such Shares shall rank *pari passu* with the other shares of the same class in issue at the date of allotment.

9.5 When an Option is exercised only in part, the balance shall remain exercisable on the same terms as originally applied to the whole Option and a new option certificate shall be issued accordingly by the Company as soon as possible after the partial exercise.

10. ADMINISTRATION AND AMENDMENT

10.1 The Scheme shall be administered by the Board whose decision on all disputes shall be final.

10.2 The Board may from time to time amend these Rules provided that
    i. no amendment may materially affect an Option Holder as regards an Option granted prior to the amendment being made
    ii. no amendment may be made which would make the terms on which Options may be granted materially more generous or would increase the limit specified in Rule 5.1 without the prior approval of the Company in general meeting and
    iii. no amendment shall have effect until approved by the Board of Inland Revenue.

10.3 The cost of establishing and operating the Scheme shall be borne by the Participating Companies in such proportions as the Board shall determine.

10.4 The Board may establish a committee consisting of not less than three Board members to whom any or all of its powers in relation to the Scheme may be delegated. The Board may at any time dissolve the Committee, alter its constitution or direct the manner in which it shall act.

10.5 Any notice or other communication under or in connection with the Scheme may be given by the Company either personally or by post and to the Company either personally or by post to the secretary; items sent by post shall be pre-paid and shall by deemed to have been received 72 hours after posting.

10.6 The Company shall at all times keep available sufficient authorised and unissued Shares to satisfy the exercise to the full extent still possible of all Options which have neither lapsed nor been fully exercised, taking account of any other obligations of the Company to issue unissued Shares.

Notes

1. Insert name of company.
2. This definition is of use only if the scheme shares are quoted on the Stock Exchange.
3. Appropriate only where the scheme shares are quoted on the Stock Exchange.
4. Appropriate only where the scheme shares are not quoted on the Stock Exchange.
5. The description of the scheme shares should be inserted here.
6. This sentence may be omitted if provision is made in the Rules for options to be granted under seal. This is to ensure that the Option Holder has an enforceable right.

7. These provisions are not required for Inland Revenue approval. They are designed to protect existing shareholders and each company must decide for itself what, if any, limits it needs to impose.
8. The provision appropriate to the company should be chosen.

Appendix 8

Savings-Related Share Option Scheme – Inland Revenue Specimen Rules

(Crown copyright. Reproduced by kind permission of the Controller of Her Majesty's Stationery Office)

Where indicated, reference should also be made to the numbered notes at the end of this appendix.

Rules of the [................]¹
Savings-Related Share Option Scheme

1.1 DEFINITIONS

In these Rules the following words and expressions shall have the following meanings:

'Adoption Date'	the date on which the Scheme is adopted by the Company in general meeting.
'Announcement Date'	the date on which the annual or half-yearly results of the Company are announced.
'Associated Company'	the meaning that the expression bears in paragraph 23 of Schedule 9 by virtue of Section 187 (2) of ICTA 1988]
'Auditors'	the auditors for the time being of the Company (acting as experts, not as arbitrators).
'Board'	the Board of Directors of the Company or, except in Rule 10.4, a duly constituted committee thereof.
'Bonus Date'	either: i. where pursuant to Rules 2 and 3 the repayment under the Savings Contract is taken as including the maximum bonus, the earliest date on which the maximum bonus is payable, or

	ii. in any other case, the earliest date on which a bonus (the 'standard' bonus) is payable under the Savings Contract.
'Company'	[................]¹
'Control'	has the same meaning as in Section 840 of ICTA 1988.
'Date of Grant'	the date on which an application for an Option is, was, or may be accepted in accordance with Rule 4.
'Eligible Employee'	any director or employee of any Participating Company who normally devotes to his duties 25 hours or more per week, had on the day preceding the date of issue of the relevant invitations pursuant to Rule 2.1 been such a director or employee for [................]⁶ or more years, and is chargeable to tax in respect of his office or employment under Case I of Schedule E, and any other director or employee of any Participating Company nominated by the Board to be an Eligible Employee.
'ICTA 1988'	The Income and Corporation Taxes Act 1988.
'Market Value'	[on any day the average of the middle market quotations of a Share as derived from The Stock Exchange Daily Official List for the three immediately preceding dealing days.]² [on any day the market value of a Share determined in accordance with the provisions of Part VIII of the Capital Gains Tax Act 1979 and agreed in advance for the purposes of the Scheme with the Inland Revenue Shares Valuation Division.]³
'Option'	a right to subscribe for Shares granted (or to be granted) in accordance with the Rules of this Scheme.
'Participating Company'	the Company and any other company of which the Company has Control and which has been nominated by the Board as a Participating Company.

'Savings Contract'	a contract under a certified contractual savings scheme, within the meaning of Section 326 of the Act and which has been approved by the Board of Inland Revenue for the purposes of Schedule 9.
'Schedule 9'	Schedule 9 to the ICTA 1988.
'the Scheme'	the savings-related share option scheme constituted and governed by these rules as from time to time amended.
'Share'	an [ordinary][7] share in the capital of the Company which satisfies the conditions specified in paragraphs 10 to 14 inclusive of Schedule 9.
'Subscription Price'	the price at which each Share subject to an Option may be acquired on the exercise of that Option being, subject to Rule 8, the higher of:

    i. the nominal value of a Share, and
    ii. 80% of the Market Value of a Share on the day the invitation to apply for that Option was issued pursuant to Rule 2.

'Subsisting Option'	An Option which has neither lapsed nor been exercised.

1.2 INTERPRETATION

In this Scheme, except insofar as the context otherwise requires:
    i. words denoting the singular shall include the plural and vice versa
    ii. words denoting the masculine gender shall include the feminine gender
    iii. reference to any enactment shall be construed as a reference to that enactment as from time to time amended, extended or re-enacted.

2. INVITATIONS TO APPLY FOR OPTIONS

2.1 The Board may invite every Eligible Employee to apply for the grant of an Option to acquire Shares in the Company on any one occasion within each of the following periods:
    i. a period of four weeks commencing four weeks following the approval of the Scheme by the Board of Inland Revenue pursuant to Schedule 9.
    ii. a period of four weeks commencing two weeks after each Announcement Date provided that no invitation may be made after the tenth anniversary of the Adoption Date.

2.2 Each invitation shall specify:
    i. the date, being 14 days after the issue of the invitation, by which an application must be made

  ii. the Subscription Price at which Shares may be acquired on the exercise of any Option granted in response to the application and

  iii. the maximum permitted aggregate monthly savings contribution, being the lesser of the maximum specified in paragraph 24 of Schedule 9 and such sum (being a multiple of £1 and not less than £10) as the Board decides shall apply to every Eligible Employee in respect of that invitation.

2.3 Each invitation shall be accompanied by a proposal form for a Savings Contract and an application form which shall provide for the applicant to state:

  i. the monthly savings contribution (being a multiple of £1 and not less than £10) which he wishes to make under the related Savings Contract,

  ii. that his proposed monthly savings contribution, when added to any monthly savings contributions then being made under any other Savings Contract linked to an option granted under the Scheme or any other scheme approved under Schedule 9, will not exceed the maximum permitted aggregate monthly savings contribution specified in the invitation,

  iii. whether, for the purpose of determining the number of Shares over which an Option is to be granted, the repayment under the Savings Contract is to be taken as including the maximum bonus, the standard bonus or no bonus,

and to authorise the Board to enter on the Savings Contract proposal form such monthly savings contribution, not exceeding the maximum stated on the application form, as shall be determined pursuant to Rule 3 below.

2.4 Each application shall be deemed to be for an Option over the largest whole number of Shares which can be bought at the Subscription Price with the expected repayment under the related Savings Contract at the appropriate Bonus Date.

3. SCALING DOWN

If the Board receives valid applications for Options over an aggregate number of Shares which exceeds the limit determined pursuant to Rule 5.2 below in respect of that invitation, then the following steps shall be carried out successively to the extent necessary to eliminate the excess:

  i. the excess over £10 of the monthly savings contribution chosen by each applicant shall be reduced pro rata to the extent necessary;

  ii. each election for the maximum bonus to be included in the repayment under the Savings Contract shall be deemed to be an election for only the standard bonus to be so included;

  iii. in the repayment under the Savings Contract shall be deemed to be an election for no bonus to be so included;

iv. applications will be selected by lot, each based on a monthly savings contribution of £10 and the inclusion of no bonus in the repayment under the Savings Contract.

Each application shall be deemed to have been modified or withdrawn in accordance with the application of the foregoing provisions and the Board shall complete each Savings Contract proposal form to reflect any reduction in monthly savings contributions resulting therefrom.

4. GRANT OF OPTIONS

Not later than the thirtieth day following [the earliest of the three dealing days referred to in the definition of Market Value] [the day on which invitations were issued pursuant to Rule 2] the Board shall grant to each applicant who is still an Eligible Employee and is not precluded from participation in the Scheme by virtue of paragraph 8 of Schedule 9 an Option over the number of Shares for which, pursuant to Rule 2.4 and subject to Rule 3, he is deemed to have applied.

As soon as possible after Options have been granted the Board shall issue a certificate of option in respect of each Option in such form, not inconsistent with these Rules, as the Board may determine.

No Option may be transferred, assigned or charged and any purported transfer, assignment or charge shall cause the Option to lapse forthwith. Each Option certificate shall carry a statement to this effect.

5. LIMITATIONS ON GRANTS

5.1 No Option shall be granted pursuant to Rule 4 above if such grant would result in the aggregate of
   i. the number of Shares over which Subsisting Options have been granted under this Scheme and
   ii. the number of Shares which have been issued on the exercise of Options granted under this Scheme and
   iii. the number of Shares over which Subsisting Options have been granted under any other share option scheme during the period of 10 years ending on the relevant Date of Grant and
   iv. the number of Shares which have been issued pursuant to any other employee share scheme (including a share option scheme) during the period of 10 years ending on the relevant Date of Grant exceeding 5% of the number of Shares then in issue.]4

5.2 The Board may, before issuing invitations on any occasion, determine a limit on the number of Shares which are to be available in respect of that invitation in order to ensure that Shares remain available for subsequent invitations.

5.3 No Option shall be granted to an Eligible Employee if the monthly savings contribution under the related Savings Contract, when added to the monthly savings contribution then being made under any other

Savings Contract, would exceed the maximum specified in paragraph 24 of Schedule 9.

6. EXERCISE OF OPTIONS

6.1 Subject to Rule 9 below any Subsisting Option may be exercised in whole or in part at any time following the earliest of the following events:
   i. the relevant Bonus Date;
   ii. the death of the Option Holder;
   iii. the Option Holder ceasing to be a director or employee of any Participating Company by reason of injury, disability, redundancy within the meaning of the Employment Protection (Consolidation) Act 1978 or retirement on reaching pensionable age within the meaning of Schedule 20 to the Social Security Act 1975 or any other age at which he is bound to retire in accordance with the terms of his contract of employment;
   iv. the Option Holder ceasing to be a director or employee of any Participating Company by reason only that –
     a. that office or employment is in a company of which the Company ceases to have Control, or
     b. that office or employment relates to a business or part of a business which is transferred to a person who is neither an Associated Company (as defined in Section 416 of ICTA 1988) nor a company of which the Company has Control;
   v. the Option Holder ceasing to be a director or employee of any Participating Company more than three years after the Date of Grant of the relative Option by reason of [.....].[5]

6.2 An Option shall lapse on the earliest of the following events:
   i. except where the Option Holder has died, the expiry of six months following the Bonus Date;
   ii. where the Option Holder died during the six months following the Bonus Date, the first anniversary of the Bonus Date;
   iii. where the Option Holder has died before the Bonus Date, the first anniversary of his death;
   iv. unless the Option Holder has died, the expiry of six months after the Option has become exercisable by virtue of paragraph (iii) of Rule 6.1;
   v. the expiry of six months after the Option has become exercisable by virtue of paragraph (iv) or (v) of Rule 6.1 or in accordance with Rule 7;
   vi. the Option Holder ceasing to be a director or employee of any Participating Company in circumstances in which the Option does not become exercisable;
   vii. the Option Holder being adjudicated bankrupt.

6.3 If an Option Holder continues to be employed by a Participating Company after the date on which he reaches pensionable age within the meaning of Schedule 20 to the Social Security Act 1975 he may exercise any Subsisting Option within six months following that date.

6.4 No person shall be treated for the purposes of this Rule 6 as ceasing to be employed by any Participating Company until he is no longer employed by the Company, any Associated Company or Company of which the Company has Control.

7. TAKEOVERS AND LIQUIDATIONS

7.1 If any person obtains Control of the Company as a result of making:

    i. a general offer to acquire the whole of the issued ordinary share capital of the Company which is made on a condition such that if it is satisfied the person making the offer will have Control of the Company, or

    ii. a general offer to acquire all the shares in the Company which are of the same class as the Shares,

then any Subsisting Option may be exercised within six months of the time when the person making the offer has obtained Control of the Company and any condition subject to which the offer is made has been satisfied.

7.2 If under Section 425 of the Companies Act 1985 or Article 418 of the Companies (Northern Ireland) Order 1986[8] the Court sanctions a compromise or arrangement proposed for the purposes of or in connection with a scheme for the reconstruction of the Company or its amalgamation with any other company or companies, any Subsisting Option may be exercised within six months of the Court sanctioning the compromise or arrangement.

7.3 If any person becomes bound or entitled to acquire shares in the Company under Section 428 or 429 of the said Act of 1985 or Articles 421 to 423 of the Law Order of 1986[8] any Subsisting Option may be exercised at any time when the person remains so bound or entitled.

7.4 If as a result of the events specified in Rules 7.1 or 7.2 a company has obtained Control of the Company, or if a company has become bound or entitled as mentioned in Rule 7.3, the Option Holder may, by agreement with that other company (the 'Acquiring Company'), within the Appropriate Period, release each subsisting option (the 'Old Option') for a new option which satisfies the conditions that it:

    i. is over shares in the Acquiring Company or some other company falling within paragraph (b) or paragraph (c) of Paragraph 10, Schedule 9, which satisfy the conditions specified in paragraphs 10 to 14 of Schedule 9;

    ii. is a right to acquire such number of such Shares as has on acquisition of the new Option an aggregate Market Value equal to the aggregate market value of the shares subject to the Old Option on its release;

iii. has a Subscription Price per Share such that the aggregate price payable on complete exercise equals the aggregate price which would have been payable on complete exercise of the Old Option; and

iv. is otherwise identical in terms to the Old Option.

The New Option shall, for all other purposes of this scheme, be treated as having been acquired at the same time as the Old Option.

Where any New Options are granted pursuant to this clause 7.4, Rules 7, 8, 9, 10.1 and 10.3 to 10.6 shall, in relation to the New Options, be construed as if reference to the Company and to the Shares were references to the Acquiring Company or, as the case may be, to the other company to whose shares the New Options relate, and to the shares in that other company, but references to Participating Company shall continue to be construed as if references to the Company were references to [.................]¹.

7.5 If the Company passes a resolution for voluntary winding up, any Subsisting Option may be exercised within six months of the passing of the resolution.

7.6 For the purposes of this Rule 7 (other than 7.4) a person shall be deemed to have obtained Control of a company if he and others acting in concert with him have together obtained Control of it.

7.7 The exercise of an Option pursuant to the preceding provisions of this Rule 7 shall be subject to the provisions of Rule 9 below.

7.8 Where in accordance with 7.4 Subsisting Options are released and New Options granted the New Options shall not be exercisable in accordance with Rules 7.1, 7.2, and 7.3 above by virtue of the event by reason of which the New Options were granted.

8. VARIATION OF SHARE CAPITAL

In the event of any capitalisation or rights issue or any consolidation, subdivision or reduction of capital by the Company, the number of Shares subject to any Option and the Subscription Price for each of those Shares shall be adjusted in such manner as the Auditors confirm to be fair and reasonable provided that:

i. the aggregate amount payable on the exercise of an Option in full is neither materially changed nor increased beyond the expected repayment under the Savings Contract at the appropriate Bonus Date

ii. the Subscription Price for a Share is not reduced below its nominal value

iii. no adjustment shall be made without the prior approval of the Board of Inland Revenue and

iv. following the adjustment the Shares continue to satisfy the conditions specified in paragraphs 10 to 14 inclusive of Schedule 9.

9. MANNER OF EXERCISE OF OPTIONS

9.1 No Option may be exercised by an individual at any time when he is, or by the personal representatives of an individual who at the date of his death was, precluded by paragraph 8 of Schedule 9 from participating in the Scheme.

9.2 No Option may be exercised at any time when the shares which may thereby be acquired are not Shares as defined in Rule 1.1.

9.3 An Option may only be exercised over the number of Shares which may be purchased with the sum obtained by way of repayment under the related Savings Contract.

9.4 An Option shall be exercised by the Option holder, or as the case may be his personal representatives, giving notice to the Company in writing of the number of Shares in respect of which he wishes to exercise the Option accompanied by the appropriate payment (which shall not exceed the sum obtained by way of repayment under the related Savings Contract) and the relevant option certificate, and shall be effective on the date of its receipt by the Company.

9.5 Shares shall be allotted and issued pursuant to a notice of exercise within 30 days of the date of exercise. Save for any rights determined by reference to a date preceding the date of allotment, such Shares shall rank *pari passu* with the other Shares of the same class in issue at the date of allotment.

9.6 When an Option is exercised only in part, it shall lapse to the extent of the unexercised balance.

9.7 For the purposes of Rules 9.3 and 9.4 above, any repayment under the Savings Contract shall exclude the repayment of any contribution the due date for payment of which falls more than one month after the date on which repayment is made.

10. ADMINISTRATION AND AMENDMENT

10.1 The Scheme shall be administered by the Board whose decision on all disputes shall be final.

10.2 The Board may from time to time amend these Rules provided that:
   i. no amendment may materially affect an Option Holder as regard an Option granted prior to the amendment being made
   ii. no amendment may be made which would make the terms on which Options may be granted materially more generous or would increase the limit specified in Rule 5.1 without the prior approval of the Company in general meeting and
   iii. no amendment shall have effect until approved by the Board of Inland Revenue.

10.3 The cost of establishing and operating the Scheme shall be borne by the Participating Companies in such proportions as the Board shall determine.

10.4 The Board may establish a committee consisting of not less than three members to whom any or all of its powers in relation to the Scheme may be delegated. The Board may at any time dissolve the Committee, alter its constitution or direct the manner in which it shall act.

10.5 Any notice or other communication under or in connection with the Scheme may be given by the Company either personally or by post and to the Company either personally or by post to the secretary; items sent by post shall be pre-paid and shall be deemed to have been received 72 hours after posting.

10.6 The Company shall at all times keep available sufficient authorised and unissued Shares to satisfy the exercise to the full extent still possible of all Options which have neither lapsed nor been fully exercised, taking account of any other obligations of the Company to issue unissued Shares.

Notes

1. Insert name of company.
2. Appropriate only where the scheme shares are listed in The Stock Exchange Daily Official List. (This does not include the shares of companies traded on the Unlisted Securities Market or on NASDAQ, the over-the-counter market).
3. Appropriate where the scheme shares are not listed in The Stock Exchange Daily Official List.
4. These provisions are not required for Inland Revenue approval. They are designed to protect existing shareholders and each company must decide for itself what, if any, limits should be imposed.
5. If an Option Holder leaves employment for reasons other than those specified in Rule 6.1(iii), any option which has been held for more than three years at the date of leaving may be exercised if the Rules so allow. The company should decide in what circumstances, if any, such exercise should be permitted and specify these in Rule 6.1(v).
6. Any period not longer than 4 years 334 days may be chosen so that the interval between the beginning of the period and the date of grant does not exceed 5 years.
7. The description of the scheme shares should be inserted here.
8. The provision appropriate to the company should be chosen.

Appendix 9

Profit-Sharing Scheme – Inland Revenue Specimen Trust Deed and Rules

(Crown Copyright. Reproduced by kind permission of the Controller of Her Majesty's Stationery Office)

The Specimen Trust Deed and Rules have been updated by Stoy Hayward to take account of the consolidation of legislation in the Income and Corporation Taxes Act 1988.

This Trust Deed is made [date] between [company], whose registered office is at [address] of the one part (hereinafter called 'the Company'), and [names and addresses of trustees] (hereinafter called 'the Trustees' which expression shall where the context so admits include the Trustees or Trustee for the time being of the Scheme) of the other part.

Whereas:

A. The Company wishes to establish a profit-sharing scheme known as [name of scheme] (hereinafter called 'the Scheme') in accordance with the provisions of Section 186 of the Income and Corporation Taxes Act 1988 and constituting an employee share scheme for the purpose of providing funds to the Trustees from time to time to enable Shares in the capital of the Company which satisfy the provisions of the Act to be acquired by the Trustees and subsequently to be appropriated by the Trustees to such directors and employees of the Participating Companies (as defined in the Rules hereinafter referred to) as shall be eligible in accordance with the Rules of the Scheme to participate herein.
B. The Scheme is established pursuant to an ordinary resolution of the Company passed on [date].
C. The Trustees have agreed to be the first Trustees of the Scheme.

Now this Deed witnesseth as follows:

1. *Definitions*
The definitions contained in the Rules as set out in the Schedule hereto or as amended from time to time as therein provided shall apply to this Deed.

2. *Trustees' Funds*

Subject to the further provisions of this Deed and the Rules, the Trustees shall apply the sums of money transferred to them in the acquisition of Scheme Shares or the payment of expenses or other liabilities (as the case may be) in accordance with the Rules, and shall hold the Scheme Shares once appropriated and all other property deriving therefrom upon trust for the Participants to whom those Scheme Shares have been appropriated, and shall apply and deal with the same in accordance with the Rules.

3. *Investment*

The Trustees shall invest any monies from time to time held by them and not required immediately for the purchase of Scheme Shares in such short-term investments as they may think appropriate. Any income arising on any such short-term investments shall be used for the purpose of acquiring further Scheme Shares or to meet taxation or other liabilities or expenses incurred from time to time in the operation and administration of the Scheme.

4. *Trustees' Obligations*

4.1 The Trustees shall appropriate the Scheme Shares held by them to Eligible Employees in accordance with the Rules.

4.2 As soon as practicable after any Scheme Shares have been appropriated by the Trustees to a Participant in accordance with the Rules the Trustees shall give the Participant notice in writing of the appropriation specifying the number and description of Scheme Shares so appropriated and stating their Initial Market Value and the date on which such Scheme Shares were so appropriated.

4.3 The Trustees shall not during the Period of Retention dispose of any Scheme Shares (whether by transfer to the Participant or otherwise) except as mentioned in paragraphs 1(a), (b) or (c) of Schedule 10 to the Act.

4.4 The Trustees shall not after the end of the Period of Retention and before the Release Date dispose of any Scheme Shares appropriated to a Participant except pursuant to a direction given by or on behalf of the Participant or any person in whom the beneficial interest in his scheme shares is for the time being vested and by a transaction which would not involve a breach of the Participant's obligation under paragraphs 2(2) (c) or (d) of Schedule 9 of the Act.

4.5 The Trustees, subject to their obligations under paragraph 7 of Schedule 10 to the Act and to any such direction as is referred to in Paragraph 4(2) of Schedule 10 to the Act, shall pay over to the Participant any money or money's worth received by them in respect of, or by reference to, any of his Scheme Shares other than money's worth consisting of new shares within the meaning of paragraph 5 of Schedule 10 to the Act and shall deal only pursuant to a direction given by or on behalf of the Participant or any person in whom the beneficial interest in his shares is for the time being vested with any right conferred in respect of any of his Scheme Shares to be allotted other shares securities or rights of any description.

4.6 The Trustees shall maintain such records as may be necessary to enable the Trustees to carry out their obligations under paragraph 7 of Schedule 10 to the Act and, where the Participant becomes liable to income tax under Schedule E by reason of the occurrence of any event, shall inform him of any facts relevant to determining that liability.

4.7 The Trustees shall at all times comply with their obligations to make payments to any of the Participating Companies and to make PAYE deductions contained in paragraph 7 of Schedule 10 to the Act.

4.8 The Trustees will take all reasonable steps to notify Participants of the principal terms of any offer, compromise, arrangement or scheme affecting any of a Participant's Appropriated Shares.

In the absence of any direction from a Participant concerning how the Trustees should act in respect of his Shares following any offer, compromise, arrangement or scheme the Trustees shall not take any action in respect thereof.

5. *Trustees' Regulations*

5.1 The number of Trustees hereof shall be not less than two persons unless a company is appointed as sole Trustee and if at any time the number of the Trustees shall fall below such limits the surviving or continuing Trustee shall have power to act only for the purpose of doing all things necessary to concur in or secure the appointment of a new Trustee or Trustees.

5.2 Subject to 5.1 above any Trustee may at any time resign office by giving notice in writing to the Company.

5.3 The Company may at any time and without giving any reason therefor by Deed appoint a new or additional Trustee or Trustees or may remove from office any Trustee and appoint a new Trustee or Trustees in the place of any Trustee who is removed from office or whose office is vacated for any reason and any such new or additional Trustee or (as the case may require) the existing Trustees shall thereupon execute such documents and do such things as may be necessary to give proper effect to such appointment or removal.

5.4 At all times at least one of the Trustees of the Scheme shall be resident in the United Kingdom.

5.5 A person shall not be disqualified from acting as a Trustee of the Scheme by reason of the fact that he is or has been an employee of a Participating Company or is or has been a Participant.

6. *The Participating Companies to Indemnify the Trustees*

The Participating Companies hereby covenant with the Trustees that they shall indemnify the Trustees and keep them indemnified against all claims, losses, expenses and demands whatsoever which may arise out of or in connection with the Scheme other than claims which may arise from their own negligence, fraud or misfeasance.

7. *Trustees to Rely on Company Information*

The Trustees shall be entitled to rely without further enquiry on all information supplied to them by the Participating Companies for the purposes of the Scheme and in particular but without prejudice to the generality of the foregoing any notice given by the Participating Companies to the Trustees in respect of the eligibility of any person to become or remain a Participant in the Scheme shall be conclusive in favour of the Trustees.

8. *Trustees' Meetings*

The Trustees shall meet together at such time as shall be necessary for the administration of the Scheme and all decisions relating to the Scheme made by a majority of the Trustees present and any meeting of the Trustees of which due notice has been given to all the Trustees (and at which at least two of the Trustees shall be present) shall be as effective for all purposes as if such decisions had been the unanimous decisions of all the Trustees. A resolution in writing signed by all the Trustees shall be as effective as any resolution duly passed at a meeting of the Trustees.

9. *Trustees Exonerated from Liability*

In the administration of the Scheme no Trustee shall be liable for any loss arising by reason of the negligence or fraud of any agent employed by him or by any of the other Trustees or by reason of any mistake or omission made in good faith by any of the Trustees hereof or by reason of any other matter or thing except negligence, fraud or misfeasance on the part of the Trustee who is sought to be made liable.

10. *Termination of Scheme*

10.1 The perpetuity period applicable to this Deed shall be the period of 80 years from the date hereof.

10.2 The Scheme shall be terminated at the end of the said perpetuity period or if earlier upon the date on which the Board shall resolve to terminate the Scheme.

10.3 On the date of termination any unrestricted shares in the Company registered in the names of the Trustees to which any Participant is absolutely entitled shall be immediately transferable to such Participant subject to the requirements of paragraph 2(2) of Schedule 9 and paragraph 1(1) of Schedule 10 to the Act relating to the retention and disposal of shares. Any other assets representing the Trust Property shall be paid to the Participating Companies in proportion to the total monies provided by each of them to the Trustees.

11. *Subsidiaries*

Any company which is for the time being a Subsidiary may with the consent of the Company and the Trustees be and become a party to these presents and the Scheme by entering into a Deed agreeing to be bound in all respects by this Deed and Rules for so long as such company is a Subsidiary.

A company which ceases to be a Subsidiary shall cease forthwith to participate in the Scheme. The Board may also determine that any Subsidiary, which is a Participating Company shall cease to participate (provided that paragraph 2(3)(b) of Schedule 9 to the Act is not thereby breached) and such cessation shall not affect those rights of any Participants employed by such Subsidiary to Shares appropriated before such cessation.

12. *Costs and Expenses*

The costs and expenses of the preparation and execution of this Deed and Rules and all ancillary documentation and of the management and administration of the Scheme (including the expenses of any Trustee hereof) shall be borne by the Participating Companies except insofar as the same shall be chargeable to any one or more of the Participants.

13. *Amendments*

The Company may at any time by Deed modify the trusts of this Deed with the prior approval of the Board of Inland Revenue.

14. This Deed and the Rules shall be governed by and construed in all respects in accordance with English Law.

IN WITNESS whereof the company has hereunto affixed its Common Seal and the Trustees have hereunto set their hands and seals the day and year first before written.

THE COMMON SEAL OF)
    was hereunto)
affixed in the presence of:-)

    Director

    Secretary

SIGNED SEALED AND DELIVERED)
by the said)
    in the presence of:-)

SIGNED SEALED AND DELIVERED)
by the said)
    in the presence of:-)

THE SCHEDULE above referred to
RULES OF THE [Name of Scheme]

1. *Definitions*
In the Trust Deed and the Rules:-

1.1 The following words and expressions bear the following meanings:-

'The Act'	The Income and Corporation Taxes Act 1988 (as amended).
'Announcement Date'	The date on which the Company announces the results for the relevant accounting period.
'Appropriate'	Formally to vest a beneficial interest (subject to the provisions of the Deed) in specific shares in an Eligible Employee pursuant to these Rules.
'Appropriated Shares'	In relation to any Participant, such securities as have been appropriated or are deemed to have been appropriated to him under the Scheme and are for the time being held by the Trustees and, where the context so admits, includes any new Shares within the meaning of Rule 7.3.
'Appropriation Date'	In relation to any Scheme Shares, the date upon which those Scheme Shares are appropriated to a Participant pursuant to the Scheme.
'Approved Scheme'	A profit-sharing scheme which is for the time being approved in accordance with Part I of Schedule 9 to the Act.
'The Board'	The Board of Directors of the Company or a duly constituted Committee thereof.
'The Company'	[Name of company setting up this Scheme]
'Eligible Earnings'	In relation to an Eligible Employee on any Appropriation Date, the annual rate of basic salary (excluding any supplements or other emoluments as may be payable in addition to basic salary) payable by the Participating Companies on the last day in the Financial Year immediately preceding the Financial Year in which the Appropriation Date falls.
'Eligible Employee'	Any person who is eligible to participate in the scheme in accordance with Rule 2.
'Financial Year'	A financial year of the company as that term is defined in Section 742 of the Companies Act 1985.

'Initial Market Value'   In relation to any Scheme Shares, the
market value of those Scheme Shares
determined in accordance with Section
150(1) of the Capital Gains Tax Act 1979 as
at the Appropriation Date of those Scheme
Shares and as agreed in advance between
the Trustees and the Shares Valuation
Division of the Capital Taxes Office of the
Inland Revenue for the purposes of the
Scheme.

Provided that, if at the Appropriation
Date Shares have been admitted to the
Official List of the Stock Exchange, the
Initial Market Value of a Share shall be
taken as the average of the middle market
prices as ascertained from the Daily
Official List of the Stock Exchange of a
Share over the 5 consecutive dealing days
ending immediately prior to the relevant
Appropriation Date or ending on such
earlier date (not being earlier than 25 days
preceding such Appropriation Date) as the
Trustees may agree in writing with the
Board of Inland Revenue.

'Participant'   Any Eligible Employee to whom the
Trustees have appropriated Scheme
Shares and for whom they hold the Shares
on Trust.

'Participating Companies'   The Company and such of the
Subsidiaries as, for the time being, are
nominated by the Board to be
Participating Companies and are bound
by the provisions of the Scheme and Trust
Deed.

'Period of Retention'   In relation to any of a Participant's Scheme
Shares, the period beginning on the
Appropriation Date of those Scheme
Shares and ending on the second
anniversary of that date, or, if it is earlier:-

a. the date on which the Participant
ceases to be an employee or director of
the Participating Companies by reason
of injury or disability or Redundancy;

b. the date on which the Participant reaches pensionable age (currently 65 years for a man and 60 years for a woman) as defined in Schedule 20 to the Social Security Act 1975;

c. the date of the Participant's death.

d. Such other meaning ascribed thereto by paragraph 2 of Schedule 10 to the Act.

'Redundancy' Dismissal by reason of redundancy within the meaning of Part VI of the Employment Protection (Consolidation) Act 1978.

'The Release Date' In relation to any of a Participant's Scheme Shares, the fifth anniversary of the Appropriation Date of those Scheme Shares or such other meaning ascribed thereto by Section 187(2) of the Act.

'The Relevant Amount' The meaning ascribed thereto by Section 187(2) of the Act.

'The Rules The rules set out in this Schedule as amended from time to time in accordance with the provisions herein contained.

'The Scheme' [Name of Scheme]

'Scheme Shares' Shares subscribed for or purchased by the Trustees pursuant to the Scheme together with all shares subsequently acquired by the Trustees by virtue of their holding such Shares, exercising any rights attaching thereto or accepting any offer made to the holders of such shares and any reference to a Participant's Scheme Shares is, subject to Rule 7 (d), a reference to the Scheme Shares which have been appropriated to him by the Trustees.

'Shares' Ordinary Shares in the capital of the Company which comply with the conditions set out in paragraphs 10, 11, 12 and 14 of Schedule 9 to the Act.

'Subsidiary' Any company which is for the time being controlled by the Company within the meaning of Section 840 of the Act.

'Trust Property'	Any shares, money and other property from time to time in the name of, transferred to or held by the Trustees or under their control and subject to the terms of this Deed and the Rules.
'The Trustees'	The trustee or trustees for the time being of the Scheme.
'Year of Assessment'	A year beginning on any 6 April and ending on the following 5 April.

1.2 Reference to any Act or Part, Chapter or Section thereof (including 'the Act' as herein defined) shall include any statutory modification, amendment or re-enactment thereof for the time being in force.

1.3 Words of the masculine gender shall include the feminine and vice versa and words in the singular shall include the plural and vice versa unless, in either case, the context otherwise requires or it is otherwise stated.

2. *Eligibility*

2.1 Any person who fulfils the following conditions, namely:-

   a. he is a director or employee of a Participating Company who is required to devote to his duties not less than 25 hours per week (excluding meal breaks), and

   b. he has completed not less than [period not to exceed five years] of continuous employment as such, and

   c. he is chargeable to income tax in respect of his employment under Case I of Schedule E

   shall be entitled as of right to participate in the Scheme at an Appropriate Date.

   Provided that:-

   a. he is not ineligible to have Scheme Shares appropriated to him by virtue of the provisions of paragraphs 8 and 35 of Schedule 9 to the Act; and

   b. he has before any Scheme Shares are appropriated to him delivered a contract of participation with the Company in terms which include the observance of the four conditions (a), (b), (c) and (d) set out in paragraph 2(2) of Schedule 9 to the Act and which is in the form substantially as set out in Appendix II.

2.2 a. As soon as practicable after the Announcement Date the Company shall identify all Eligible Employees who are not then participating in the Scheme and all employees who at the next Appropriation Date are expected to be Eligible Employees and shall communicate in writing with each such person asking whether he wishes to be a Participant.

   b. Those Eligible Employees who wish to participate in the scheme shall within the period of 14 days after receipt of the notification referred to above or such further period as the Company shall allow return to the Company a form of acceptance duly signed agreeing the terms and conditions set out therein and in default thereof they shall not be eligible to participate.

3. *Allocation of Funds for Purchase of Shares*

3.1. The Participating Companies shall allocate funds for the purposes of the scheme on or after each Announcement Date in accordance with the provisions hereof.

3.2 The amount of the funds to be allocated as aforesaid shall be such amount (if any) as the Board may determine.

3.3 The amount determined as aforesaid shall be notified in writing to the Trustees as soon as it has been determined and shall be paid to the Trustees on the Announcement Date or as soon as possible thereafter by the Participating Companies.

The Board shall also notify the Trustees of the number of shares (if any) which are to be made available for subscription by the Trustees and the price at which those Shares are to be offered for subscription.

3.4 A Participating Company shall only pay to the Trustees such sums as are required in connection with the acquisition of Shares by the Trustees for appropriation to Eligible Employees who are for the time being in the service of that Participating Company.

3.5 The Trustees shall on or after the relevant Announcement Date but on or before the immediately following Appropriation Date apply the amount paid to them under Rule 3.3 above in subscribing for Shares of and to the extent that Shares are offered to them and at the price notified to them pursuant to sub-paragraph 3.3 above and, subject thereto, the balance shall be applied in purchasing Shares from existing shareholders.

4. *Appropriation of Scheme Shares*

4.1. The number of Scheme Shares to be appropriated by the Trustees to each Eligible Employee on any Appropriation Date on which funds have been allocated in accordance with Rule 3 above shall be determined in accordance with the following provisions:-

The entitlement of each Eligible Employee under the scheme shall be such amount as the Board shall determine expressed as:-

  i. a proportion of Eligible Earnings; and/or
  ii. a proportion of Eligible Earnings for each Period of Service; and/or
  iii. a fixed amount determined by the Board; and/or
  iv. a fixed amount determined by the Board for each Period of Service.
  Provided that:-
  a. in any year the basis of calculation of the entitlement of each Eligible Employee shall be the same;
  b. fractional amounts of the Scheme Share shall be rounded up or down at the discretion of the Trustees;

    c. the total of the Initial Market Values of the Scheme Shares appropriated to an Eligible Employee in a Year of Assessment shall not exceed the Relevant Amount.

In the context of this Rule 'Period of Service' shall mean a complete year, or such other complete period as may from time to time be specified, of continuous service as an employee of the Company and/or any Subsidiary.

4.2 The Scheme Shares to which each Eligible Employee is entitled as a result of the calculations described above will then be appropriated to him at the aggregate of their Initial Market Value but will be registered in the names of the Trustees on his behalf.

4.3 In the event that the Trustees acquire Shares for appropriation on an Appropriation Date and some of those Shares carry a right of any kind which is not carried by every other such Share then such Shares as carry such right shall so far as practicable be appropriated pro rata according to the number of Shares appropriated to each Participant on the Appropriation Date.

4.4 As soon as practicable after any Scheme Shares have been appropriated by the Trustees to a Participant in accordance with the Rules the Trustees shall give the Participant notice in writing of the appropriation specifying the number and description of Scheme Shares appropriated and stating their Initial Market Value and the date on which such Scheme Shares were appropriated.

5. *Rights and Restrictions Relating to Scheme Shares*

5.1 Scheme Shares shall subject to the provisions of the Scheme receive identical treatment and rank *pari passu* in all respects with all other shares of the same class and in particular in respect of each of the following, where applicable:-

    a. the dividend payable (provided that Scheme Shares which have been newly issued may receive, in respect of dividends payable with respect to a period beginning before the date of which such Scheme Shares were issued, treatment which is less favourable than that accorded to Shares issued before that date);

    b. repayment;

    c. the restrictions attaching to Shares; and

    d. any offer of substituted or additional Shares, securities or rights of any description in respect of Shares;

but notwithstanding the foregoing, the provisions of Rule 6 shall apply as between the Trustees and the Participants.

5.2 While Scheme Shares are held by the Trustees they shall in respect of any matter upon which the Trustees are entitled to exercise any voting right that may attach hereto, seek and comply with any direction from any of the Participants, as to the exercise of such voting rights, and in the absence of such direction refrain from voting.

5.3 Subject to the provisions of the Rules and in particular Rule 6 of the Trustees shall deal with a Participant's Scheme Shares at all times in accordance with the lawful directions given by or on behalf of that Participant or any person in whom the beneficial interest in his Scheme Shares is for the time being vested.

6. *Obligations of Participants*

6.1 Subject to Rule 6.2 every Participant shall be bound in contract with the Company:-

   a. to permit his Scheme Shares to remain in the hands of the Trustees throughout the Period of Retention, and

   b. not to assign, charge or otherwise dispose of the beneficial interest in his Scheme Shares during that period, and

   c. if he directs the Trustees to transfer the ownership of his Scheme Shares to him at any time before the Release Date, to pay to the Trustees before the transfer takes place a sum equal to income tax at the basic rate on the appropriate percentage of the locked-in value of the Scheme Shares at the time of the direction and, for this purpose, 'the appropriate percentage' and 'the locked-in value' shall be respectively defined in paragraph 3 of Schedule 10 and Section 186(5) of the Act, and

   d. not to direct the Trustees to dispose of his Scheme Shares at any time before the Release Date in any other way except by sale for the best consideration in money that can reasonably be obtained at the time of sale.

6.2 Any obligation imposed on a Participant by virtue of Rule 6.1 above shall not prevent the participant from:-

   a. directing the Trustees to accept an offer for any of his Scheme Shares (in this Rule referred to as 'the Original Shares'), if the acceptance or agreement will result in a new holding, as defined in Section 77(1)(b) of the Capital Gains Tax Act 1979, being equated with the Original Shares for the purposes of Capital Gains Tax; or

   b. directing the Trustees to agree to a transaction affecting his Scheme Shares or such of them as are of a particular class, if the transactions would be entered into pursuant to a compromise, arrangement or scheme applicable to or affecting:-

      i. all the ordinary share capital of the Company or, as the case may be, all the shares of the class in question, or

      ii. all the shares, or shares of the class in question, which are held by a class of shareholders identified otherwise than by reference to their employment or their participating in an Approved Scheme; or

   c. directing the Trustees to accept an offer of cash, with or without other assets, for his Scheme Shares if the offer forms part of a general offer which is made to holders of Shares of the same class as his or of

Shares in the Company and which is made in the first instance on a condition such that if it is satisfied the person making the offer will have control of the Company, within the meaning of Section 416 of the Act.

d. agreeing, after the expiry of the Period of Retention, to sell the beneficial interest in his Scheme Shares to the Trustees for the same consideration as, in accordance with Rule 6.1(d), would be required to be obtained for the Scheme Shares themselves.

7. *Company Reconstructions, Amalgamations, etc*

7.1 This Rule applies where there occurs in relation to any of a Participant's Scheme Shares (in this rule referred to as 'the Original Holding') a transaction (in this Rule referred to as a 'Company Reconstruction') which results in a New Holding as defined in Section 77(1)(b) of the Capital Gains Tax Act 1979 being equated with the Original Holding for the purpose of capital gains tax and in this Rule 'New Holding' has the meaning aforesaid.

7.2 Where shares are issued in the circumstances described in paragraph 5(2) of Schedule 10 to the Act those shares shall be treated for the purposes of this Rule as not forming part of the New Holding.

7.3 In this rule:-

a. 'New Shares' means shares comprised in the New Holding which were issued in respect of or otherwise represent, shares comprised in the Original Holding, and

b. 'Corresponding Shares', in relation to any New Shares, means those shares in respect of which the New Shares are issued or which the New Shares otherwise represent.

7.4 References in the Rules to a Participant's Scheme Shares shall be construed, after the time of the Company Reconstruction, as being or, as the case may be, as including references to any New Shares and for the purposes of the Rules:-

a. a Company Reconstruction shall be treated as not involving a disposal of shares comprised in the Original Holding;

b. the date on which any New Shares are to be treated as having been appropriated to the Participant shall be the Appropriation Date of the Corresponding Shares; and

c. the New Shares shall be held by the Trustees in accordance with the Scheme as if they had been so appropriated.

7.5 In the context of a New Holding any reference in this Rule to Shares includes securities or rights of any description which form part of the New Holding for the purposes of Chapter II of Part IV of the Capital Gains Tax Act 1979.

8. *Rights Issues*

In the event of the Company making an offer to its ordinary shareholders on a rights basis such offer shall be extended to the Trustees in respect of the total number of Scheme Shares.

The Trustees shall notify each Participant concerned of the rights which are attributable to his Appropriated Shares. A Participant shall be at liberty to direct the Trustees to accept such offer in respect of all of his Scheme Shares, in which event he shall pay to the Trustees a sum of money before the expiry of the offer sufficient to enable the Trustees to subscribe for that number of Shares in respect of which the direction was made. Alternatively, a Participant may direct the Trustees to sell the whole of the rights attaching to his Scheme Shares, or, if the Trustees so permit, to sell part of such rights in order to enable the Trustees to use the proceeds of such sale to exercise other such rights of the Participant. Any shares subscribed for by the Trustees under this Rule shall be treated as New Shares under Rule 7 in relation to any Participant and any cash arising from the disposal of rights (except insofar as used to accept the offer) shall be accounted for to the Participant entitled thereto (subject to deduction of any tax unless Section 186(12) of the Act applies).

9. *Release of Shares to Participants*

Scheme Shares held by the Trustees on behalf of each Participant on the Release Date shall be transferred to that Participant as soon as reasonably practicable thereafter. In disposing of a Participant's holding of Scheme Shares which comprise Shares appropriated to him at different times Shares appropriated earlier shall, for the purposes of these rules, be treated as disposed of before those which were appropriated later.

10. *Miscellaneous*

10.1 The Board may alter or add to all or any of the provisions of the Scheme from time to time in any way they think fit.

Provided that:-

a. no alteration which would adversely prejudice to a material extent the rights attaching to any Scheme Shares appropriated to Participants shall be made nor shall any alteration be made giving the Participating Companies a beneficial interest in Scheme Shares; and

b. if the Scheme is at the time of an amendment or addition approved by the Board of Inland Revenue in accordance with Part I of Schedule 9 to the Act such amendment or addition to the scheme shall not take effect unless and until it has been approved by the Board of Inland Revenue in accordance with paragraph 4 of Schedule 9 to the Act.

10.2 Any direction to the Trustees in respect of a Participant's Appropriated Shares must be given in writing by or on behalf of the Participant or any person in whom the beneficial interest in his Shares is for the time being vested. Any notification, document, payment or other communication to a Participant shall be delivered personally or sent by post to the Participant at the address which he shall give to the Company for the purpose, or failing any such address to his last known place of abode.

10.3 The Company will provide Participants with copies of the annual report and accounts and all notices and circulars sent to the holders of Shares of the Company.

10.4 Any stamp duty payable on a transfer of a Participant's Appropriated Shares to him shall be paid by the Trustees.

11. *Limitation upon Number of Shares Available to the Scheme*

11.1 The aggregate nominal amount of all Scheme Shares issued by the Company to the Trustees and appropriated by them under the provisions of this Scheme shall not exceed [£…] and in any event shall not, in any one calendar year, exceed one per cent of the issued share capital of the Company provided always that in the event of an issue of ordinary shares…

a. credited as fully paid up by way of capitalisation of profits or reserves; or

b. by way of rights,

such limitation shall be adjusted as the Auditors for the time being of the Company shall confirm in writing to be appropriate in their opinion in order to maintain the same as a constant percentage of the issued ordinary share capital of the Company.

11.2 The initial Market Value of all Scheme Shares subscribed by the Trustees and appropriated to all Eligible Employees in respect of any Financial Year of the Company shall not exceed five per centum of the profits (before taxation and extraordinary items) for the Company and its Subsidiaries for that Financial Year.

Appendix I to the Rules: Offer of Participation in the Employee Share Scheme

This letter formally offers you participation in the [name of scheme] which is approved by the Inland Revenue under the Income and Corporation Taxes Act 1988. Your acceptance will entitle you to participate in the Scheme for the year ended […] and for future years so long as the Scheme remains in operation and approved by the Board of Inland Revenue and so long as you remain eligible to participate under the Rules of the Scheme. You may withdraw from participation at any time in accordance with the Rules of the Scheme.

Under the provisions of paragraph 2(2) of Schedule 9 to the Income and Corporation Taxes Act 1988, a copy of which is attached to this letter, participants who have been appropriated Shares under the Scheme are subject to certain restrictions mainly concerning disposals and taxation. An eligible employee is also required by the Act to bind himself in contract with the company to permit his Shares to remain with the Trustees of the Scheme for a two-year period of retention on the terms set out in paragraph 2(2) of Schedule 9, before he can participate in the Scheme.

A copy of the Trust Deed and of the Rules of the Scheme is available for your inspection at [................] and will remain so available during the operation of the Scheme. If you participate in the Scheme you will be bound by the terms of the Trust Deed and the Rules.

The formal contract required by paragraph 2(2) of Schedule 9 consists of this notice and the enclosed form of acceptance. If you wish to participate in the Scheme please complete, sign and date the form of acceptance and return it to the Company Secretary to arrive not later than [.........]. You should retain the duplicate copy.

By order of the Board
Secretary

Date

Form of acceptance and contract of participation in [name of scheme]

TO: The Company Secretary
     [Name of Company]

I accept the offer of participation in the above Scheme contained in the company's letter dated [................]. Subject to and in consideration of my being allowed to participate in the Scheme I agree to accept such Shares as are appropriated to me under the Scheme on and subject to the terms of paragraph 2(2) of Schedule 9 to the Income and Corporation Taxes Act 1988 (set out overleaf) and to be bound in contract with [name of company] in respect of all such Shares in the terms set out in the said paragraph 2(2) of Schedule 9. I further agree to be bound by the terms of the Trust Deed and the Rules.

Signed..Date ....

Full name (in block capitals) of signatory...

Private Address (in block capitals) ....

....

....

Postcode ....

Income and Corporation Taxes Act 1988

Paragraph 2(2) of Schedule 9, paragraph 1(2) of Schedule 10, paragraph 2 of Schedule 10 and Section 187(2)

Paragraph 2(2)

A profit-sharing scheme shall not be approved [under paragraph 1 above] unless the Board [of Inland Revenue] are satisfied that, whether under the terms of the scheme or otherwise, every participant in the scheme is bound in contract with the grantor concerned:

    a. to permit his shares to remain in the hands of the trustees throughout the period of retention; and

    b. not to assign, charge or otherwise dispose of his beneficial interest in his shares during that period; and

    c. if he directs the trustees to transfer the ownership of his shares to him at any time before the release date, to pay to the trustees before the transfer takes place a sum equal to income tax at the basic rate on the appropriate percentage of the locked-in value of the shares at the time of the direction; and

    d. not to direct the trustees to dispose of his shares at any time before the release date in any other way except by sale for the best consideration in money that can reasonably be obtained at the time of the sale.

Paragraph 1(2) Schedule 10

No obligation placed on the participant by virtue of paragraph 2(2)(c) of Schedule 9 above shall be construed as binding his personal representatives to pay any sums to the trustees.

Paragraph 2 Schedule 10

For the purposes of any of the relevant provisions 'the period of retention', in relation to any of a participant's shares, means the period beginning on the date on which they are appropriated to him and ending on the second anniversary of that date or, if it is earlier:-

    a. the date on which the participant ceases to be an employee or director of the grantor or in the case of a group scheme, a participating company, by reason of injury or disability or on account of his being dismissed by reason of redundancy, within the meaning of the Employment Protection (Consolidation) Act 1978; or

    b. the date on which the participant reaches pensionable age, [as defined in Schedule 20 to the Social Security Act 1975]; or

    c. the date of the participant's death;

    d. in a case where the participant's shares are redeemable shares in a workers' co-operative, the date on which the participant ceases to be employed by, or by a subsidiary of, the co-operative.

Section 187(2)

'The release date', in relation to any of the shares of a participant in a profit sharing scheme, means the fifth anniversary of the date on which they were appropriated to him.

Section 187(1)
'Grantor' in relation to any scheme means the company which has established the scheme.

Appendix II to the Rules: Share Appropriation Notice and Certificate of Beneficial Ownership

Date

(Name of Scheme)

This is to certify that [Name of Participant] ('the Participant') is the beneficial owner of [.........] Ordinary Shares of [......p] each in [name of company] and that the shares were appropriated to the Participant at an initial Market Value of [........] on [........] and are held for the Participant by the Trustees of [name of scheme] and are subject to a valid contract under paragraph 2(2) of Schedule 9 to the Income and Corporation Taxes Act 1988.

Signed

For and on behalf of the Trustees of the [Name of Scheme].

Stoy Hayward

Services of the firm

Accountancy and audit

Accounting services
Computer bureau
Company secretarial
Financial planning
Specialised audits
Statutory audits

Financial advice

Corporate finance and investigations
Entertainment industry
Litigation support
Mergers, acquisitions and flotations
Pensions planning
Personal financial planning
Property industry
Raising finance
Trust management
Venture capital

Insolvency

Administrations
Bankruptcy
Corporate rescue and reconstruction
Investigations
Liquidations
Receiverships
Voluntary arrangements

Consultancy services

Business location
Corporate strategy
Design and selection of systems
Executive recruitment
Family business unit
Feasibility studies
Franchising services
Government grants
Hotel and leisure industries
Human resource service
Implementation of systems
Management training
Marketing studies
Organisation reviews
Project management
Relocation service
Urban regeneration advice
1992 Unit

Tax

Business Expansion Scheme
Corporate taxation
International tax planning
Personal taxation
Remuneration/benefits planning
Tax investigations
UK tax planning
VAT and customs duty planning
Share scheme planning and ESOPs

Current publications

Client service brochures

Franchising
Going Bankrupt – Act Now!
Insolvency Services
International Tax Services
Litigation Support
Management Consultancy Services
Personal Financial Planning

Services to the Entertainment
   Industry
Services to the Property
   Industry
Stoy Hayward Review 1990-91
VAT and Customs Duty
1992 and Beyond

Technical publications

Audit Guide	£10.50
Business Expansion Scheme	Free
Commentary on the Budget (annual)	Free
Horwath International Tax Planning Manual	£250.00
Daily Telegraph Pensions Guide	£10.95

HAC Guide to Taxation of the Bloodstock Industry	£20.00
How to Franchise Your Business	£7.95
Inheritance Tax – a practical guide	£8.95
Model Financial Statements for Public and Private Companies	£15.95
Property Tax Planning Manual (co-published with Butterworth)	£24.95
Sources of Venture and Development Capital	Free
Tax Data Card (annual)	Free
Tax Planning (annual)	Free
The Stoy Hayward Business Tax Guide	£12.95
The Stoy Hayward USM Yearbook 1990 (co-published with Macmillan)	£95.00
VAT & Property (co-published with Butterworth)	£35.00

Surveys

Staying the course – Survival Characteristics of the Family Owned Business	£35.00
A Study to Determine the Reasons for Failure of Small Businesses in the United Kingdom	£20.00
Horwath Consulting/English Tourist Board Hotel Occupancy Survey (12 monthly surveys and 1 annual)	£250.00
Managing the family business in the UK – Summary	
– Report	£25.00
The Essence of USM Success	£40.00

Horwath Consulting Publications

Horwath Consulting Statements of Experience:	
– Tourism, Hotel, Leisure & Related Industries	
– Golf, Sports and Leisure	
– Real Estate	
An Examination of Tourism Investment Incentives	£10.00
Hotels of the Future: Strategies and Action Plan (International Hotel Association): Summary	£40.00
Full Report	£250.00
Tourism - A Portrait (published to mark Horwath's silver jubilee)	£26.25
United Kingdom Hotel Industry (annual)	£30.00
Worldwide Hotel Industry Insight/Flash	
Worldwide Hotel Industry (annual)	£40.00

United Kingdom offices

LONDON
Stoy Hayward
Stoy Hayward Consulting
Horwath Ltd
8 Baker Street
London W1M 1DA
Tel: 071-486 5888
Telex: 267716 HORWAT
Fax: 071-487 3686
LDE Box No: DE 9025
Contact: Stephen Say

BELFAST
Franklyn House
12 Brunswick Street
Belfast BT2 7GE
Tel: 0232 439009
Contact: Frank McCartan

BIRMINGHAM
Waterloo House
20 Waterloo Street
Birmingham B2 5TF
Tel: 021-643 4024
Contact: David Seccombe

BRISTOL
Oakfield House
Oakfield Grove
Clifton
Bristol BS8 2BN
Tel: 0272 237000
Contact: Richard Mannion

GLASGOW
James Sellars House
144 West George Street
Glasgow G2 2HG
Tel: 041-331 2811
Contact: Jim Wylie

LEEDS
Century House
29 Clarendon Road
Leeds LS2 9PG
Tel: 0532 341 381
Contact: Elizabeth Lennox

PETERBOROUGH
Garrick House
76-80 High Street
Old Fletton
Peterborough PE2 8DR
Tel: 0733 42444
Contact: Richard Thurlow

MANCHESTER
Peter House
St Peter's Square
Manchester M1 5BH
Tel: 061-228 6791
Contact: Stephen Halstead

NORWICH
58 Thorpe Road
Norwich NR1 1RY
Tel: 0603 660096
Contact: David White

NOTTINGHAM
Foxhall Lodge
Gregory Boulevard
Nottingham NG7 6LH
Tel: 0602 626578
Contact: Kevin Derbyshire

SUNDERLAND
19 Borough Road
Sunderland SR1 1LA
Tel: 091-565 0565
Contact: David Wrightson

International offices

Stoy Hayward is the UK member firm of Horwath International and has over 250 associated offices in the following countries:

Andorra
Argentina
Australia
Austria

Bahamas
Bahrain
Belgium
Bermuda
Bolivia
Botswana
Brazil

Canada
Cayman Islands
Channel Islands
Chile
Colombia
Cyprus

Denmark
Dominican Republic

Egypt
Ethiopia

Fiji
Finland
France

Germany
Greece
Guatemala

Haiti
Hong Kong
Hungary

Iceland

India
Ireland
Israel
Italy

Jamaica
Japan

Korea
Kuwait

Lebanon
Luxembourg

Malaysia
Mexico
Monaco
Morocco

Nepal
Netherlands
New Zealand
Nigeria

Pakistan
Panama
Portugal

Singapore
South Africa
Spain
Sri Lanka
Sweden
Switzerland
Syria

Taiwan
Thailand
Turkey

United Arab Emirates
United Kingdom
United States
Uruguay

Venezuela

Zimbabwe

Index

Accommodation provision, 47

Bonuses, sacrifice to pension, 58
  see also Profit-related pay
'Buy One, Get One Free' share schemes, 86-7

Calculation of incentive payments, 15
Cars, see Company cars
Catalogue system, 22-3
Communication
  for launch, 17-18
  in monitoring, 18
Company assets, use as perk, 44-5
Company cars, 33-42
  choice, 38
  and employee status, 34
  employer's position, 39-41
    cash purchase, 39
    contract hire versus finance leasing, 41
    hire/lease purchase, 39-41
  and income tax, 34-7
    car parking/telephones, 37-8
    and salary sacrifice, 37
    scale benefits, 35-6
  pool cars, 37
  role in incentive planning, 33
Competition for staff, 26-7
  and contracts, 27
  golden handcuffs, 29-30
    backfire example, 10-12
  golden handshakes, 30-2
    and national insurance, 32
    redundancy payments, 31-2
  golden hellos, and tax, 28-9
  leaving/staying, factors in, 26-7
  tax implications of payments, 27-8
Conferences, overseas, 24-5
Contracts
  to attract staff, 27
  specimen for profit-sharing schemes, 159
crèche facilities, 49-51

Death-in-service benefit, 59-60

Deferred bonus schemes, see Golden
  handcuffs
Design of schemes, 1-20
  appraisal meetings, 19-20
  ceremony, need for, 19
  indentifying objectives, 6-8
    goal congruence, 6
    goal incompatibility, 7-8
  launch, 17-18
  performance measure, 10-14
    choosing, 13-14
  post-launch monitoring, 18-19
  rationale for scheme, 2-5
    ceilings, 5
    discontinuance problems, 4-5
    headroom/leverage, 3
    non-financial alternatives, 3-4
    performance, factors in, 2-3
  rules checklist, 14-17
  selecting participants, 8-9
  seven stages, 1

Employee share ownership plans (ESOPS),
  92-101
  in bid defence, 97-8
  in corporate finance, 99
  as flotation alternative, 100
  for low price share capture, 98-99
  as marketmaker, 99
  qualifying schemes, 95-6
    versus non-qualifying, 96-7
  support for, 92-4
  working of, 94-5
Executive share option schemes, 83-5
  popularity, 83
  requirements, 84
  selective nature, 83

Goal congruence, 6
Golden handcuffs
  backfire example, 10-12

in share option exercising, 75
and tax, 29-30
Golden handshakes
and tax, 27-8, 30-2
redundancy payments, 31-2
and national insurance, 32
Golden hellos, and tax, 27-8, 28-9

Headroom, 3

Launch, 17-18
Leavers
inclusion in schemes, 9
scheme rules and, 16
Leaving, factors in, 26-7
Leverage, 3
Liquidations, Inland Revenue rules on
employee option schemes, 129-31
savings related option schemes, 140-41
Loans, 46-7
Long-service awards, 49
Luncheon facilities, 45

Matching offer share schemes, 86-7
Medical insurance, 46
Motivation, interactions in, 2-3
'Nagging spouse' factor, 23
National insurance, on termination
payments, 32
Non-cash schemes, 21-5
catalogue system, 22-3
'nagging spouse' factor in, 23
overseas conferences, 24-5
Taxed Award Scheme, 23-4
and visibility, 21
vouchers, 22
Nursery facilities, 49-51

Overseas conferences, 24-5

Pay, *see* Profit-related pay
Pensions, 52-63
additional benefits, 59-60
additional voluntary contributions, 57-8
capping limitation, 52
contracting out, 62-3
executive 'top hat' schemes, 56-7
final salary schemes, 54-5
money purchase schemes, 55-6
non-contributory, as golden handcuff, 30
personal, 60-61
portability, 62
rules for maximum benefits, 53
salary/bonus sacrifices, 58
unapproved arrangements, 61-2
Performance
interacting factors in, 2-3
measure choosing, 10-14
Pilot scheme, 17
Points system, 22-3

Profit-related pay, 64-70
background to introduction, 64-5
cancellation, 69
distributable pool ascertainment, 67-8
profit ascertainment, 68-9
registration, 66-7
requirements, 67
rules, 65-6
Profit-sharing schemes, 85-6
Appropriation Notice and Certificate of
Beneficial Ownership, 161
Association of British Insurers guidelines,
113-14
form of acceptance and contract of
participation, 159
and Income and Corporation Taxes Act
1988, 160-61
offer of participation, 158-9
rules, specimen, 148-58
trust deed, specimen, 144-8
Profits, windfall, 5

Recruits, inclusion in schemes, 93
Redundancy payments, and tax, 31-2
see also Leavers
Relocation, tax-free, 48
Retirement, early, and final salary pension
schemes, 55
see also Leavers; Pensions

Savings related option schemes, *see*
'Sharesave'
Selecting participants, 8-9
Self-administered pension schemes (SSAS),
57
Share incentives, 71-2
approved schemes, 83-91
Association of British Insurers Guidelines,
111-19
option schemes, 114-16
profit-sharing schemes, 113-14
savings-related schemes, 116-17
categories, 71
ceremony, need for, 80
employee option schemes, Inland
Revenue Rules, 125-33
administration/amendment, 132
applications, 128
definitions, 125-7
exercise of options, 129, 131-2
grant of options, 128-9
invitation to apply, 127-8
takeovers/liquidations, 129-31
variation of share capital, 131
employee share ownership plans (ESOPS),
92-101
in bid defence, 97-8
captive shares, 98
in corporate finance, 99
as flotation alternative, 100

as marketmaker, 99
qualifying schemes, 95-6
qualifying versus non-qualifying
    schemes, 96-7
support for, 92-4
working of, 94-5
executive share option schemes, 83-5
popularity, 83
requirements, 84
selective nature, 83
as handcuffs, 30, 75
incidence survey, 71-3
matching offer scheme, 86-7
maximising incentive, 81
National Association of Pension Funds
    Guidelines, 120-22
payment for grant of option, 80-81
phantom options, 79-80
potential rewards, 73
profit-sharing schemes, 85-6
savings related option schemes, 87-90
attractions, 88-9
building society involvement, 90
Inland Revenue Rules, 134-43
operation, 87-8
Stock Exchange Requirements, 123-4
and tax, 76-7
unapproved *versus* approved schemes,
    77-9
'Sharesave', 87-90
Association of British Insurers Guidelines,
    116-17
attractions, 88-9
building society involvement, 90-91
Inland Revenue Rules, 134-43
administration/amendment, 142-3
definitions, 134-6
exercise of options, 139-40, 142
grant of options, 138
invitation to apply, 136-7
scaling down, 137-8

takeovers/liquidations, 140-41
variation of share capital, 141-2
operation, 87-8
Sporting facilities, 49
Stock Exchange Requirements for employee
    share schemes, 123-4
Suggestion schemes, 48-9
Inland Revenue Concession, 104-5

Takeovers
employee option schemes, Inland
    Revenue rules, 129-31
employee share ownership as defence,
    97-8
savings-related option schemes, Inland
    Revenue rules, 140-41
Tax
and company cars, 34-7
car parking/telephones, 37-8
employer's position, 39-41
scale benefits, 35-6
golden handcuffs and, 29-30
golden handshakes and, 27-8, 30-2
golden hellos and, 27-8, 28-9
and overseas conferences, 25
and share incentive schemes, 76-7
unapproved *versus* approved schemes,
    77-9
Taxed Award Scheme, 23-4, 99-100
Telephones, and tax
allowances, 48
in cars, 37-8
Termination, *see* Leavers
'Top hat' pension schemes, 56-7

Visibility in non-cash schemes, 21
company cars, 33
Vouchers, 22

Windfall profits, 5